"If you want to know how to lead with charm, this book is for you. Acevedo shares his mindset as a CEO and how you can have fun at work while taking on big job responsibilities."

Eric Sim
Author of Small Actions

"As Eugene often weaves song lyrics into his writing, I was reminded of a line from an Alanis Morissette song: "You live, you learn. You love, you learn. You cry, you learn. You lose, you learn."

Why this particular song? Throughout the book, readers are invited to vicariously experience the full spectrum of Eugene's insights, lessons, and humor. These elements are skillfully distilled and clarified, offering valuable guidance for anyone looking to become a more effective leader.."

Jikyeong Kang, PhD
President and Dean, Asian Institute of Management

"ESA brilliantly combines analytical rigor with genuine empathy in leadership. His physicist's mindset shines through in his data-driven, experimental approach to banking and leadership. A true data science and AI champion, Eugene offers accessible, actionable insights for everyone. His ability to distill complex ideas into 'aha!' moments makes this an invaluable guide for aspiring leaders in the digital age."

Erika Fille Legara, PhD
Managing Director, and Chief AI and Data Officer, Center for AI Research

"Ever wished you had a career fairy godmother? This book is the next best thing. Full of witty advice and no-nonsense mentoring tips, it's like having a wise mentor in your back pocket. A must-read for anyone serious about career development and unlocking their full potential."

Yi Wen Chua
Regional Head, Investment Platform Strategic Innovation & Transformation, DBS Bank

"Eugene was my boss at Citibank in the noughties before the crisis. He was one of the kindest, well-thought-out, and understanding bosses I ever had. He mentored me, was patient with me, and I became a much better person because of him. I am a Star Wars fan and named him Eugi-one, after the greatest Jedi knights of them all."

Adam Gilmour
CEO and Founder, Gilmour Space Technologies

"The mind of a physicist, the blood of a banker, and the heart of a mentor. The pages are battle-tested leadership and life lessons gained from the trenches of leading RCBC from the frontlines. I strongly recommend that we all draw from the well of Eugene's wisdom, particularly in moments of decision that are of significant consequence."

Florentino A. Hernando
Co-founder and Executive Advisor, CEO Insights Asia

"I once saw a message from my senior manager Eugene, and it said: 'Are you ok? You seem angry.' A quick mentoring session later, I was back to my positive frame of mind. Such was the magic of his perceptiveness, his genuine interest in talent, and his passion for ensuring the right culture. He taught me how to present to a big audience, how to dress to impress and most importantly — how to succeed. I will forever be grateful to you, Eugene."

Gunjan Kathuria Kalra
APAC Commercial Bank Head, Citi

"This book provides deep insights on how to be a future leader. These include the importance of communication strategies, planning, the value of reading, mentoring and coaching others. Readers will find valuable advice about the journey of a CEO, and how one can be successful in this current world."

Dr. Robert B. Ramos
President and Chairman, CFA Society Philippines

"Empowering. Sharp. Authentic. Meet Eugene S. Acevedo and his remarkable journey in "Reinvent and Outperform." Drawing from years of experience, he shares unique perspectives and engaging personal anecdotes brimming with professional advice. Eugene masterfully navigates the nuances of modern leadership, making this book a must-read for anyone eager to make a difference."

Lito Villanueva
Founding Chairman, FinTech Alliance PH

REINVENT AND OUTPERFORM

Becoming a Better Leader

Published by

World Scientific Publishing Co. Pte. Ltd.
5 Toh Tuck Link, Singapore 596224
USA office: 27 Warren Street, Suite 401-402, Hackensack, NJ 07601
UK office: 57 Shelton Street, Covent Garden, London WC2H 9HE

Library of Congress Control Number: 2024032851

British Library Cataloguing-in-Publication Data
A catalogue record for this book is available from the British Library.

REINVENT AND OUTPERFORM
Becoming a Better Leader

ISBN 978-981-12-9892-9 (hardcover)
ISBN 978-981-98-0020-9 (paperback)
ISBN 978-981-12-9893-6 (ebook for institutions)
ISBN 978-981-12-9894-3 (ebook for individuals)

For any available supplementary material, please visit
https://www.worldscientific.com/worldscibooks/10.1142/14006#t=suppl

Desk Editor: Geysilla Jean Ortiz
Design and layout: Jimmy Low

Printed in Singapore

REINVENT AND OUTPERFORM

Becoming a Better Leader

Eugene S. Acevedo
President and CEO, Rizal Commercial Banking Corporation,
Philippines

World Scientific
NEW JERSEY • LONDON • SINGAPORE • BEIJING • SHANGHAI • HONG KONG • TAIPEI • CHENNAI • TOKYO

About the Author

Eugene S. Acevedo is the President and CEO of RCBC, one of the largest banks in the Philippines. He is a leader in digital banking and transformation and has attained multiple awards.

After completing his MBA from the Asian Institute of Management (AIM), he entered Citibank as an Executive Trainee. For over 23 years, he had assignments across Asia, the last being Managing Director and Head of Global Markets for the Hong Kong and Taiwan Cluster. Prior to that, he was based in Singapore as Head of Asia Derivatives Structuring and Sales. In addition to his business roles, he was also a sponsor of management training programs and Chairman of the Markets Asia Recruitment Committee. He later left to serve as President and CEO of Philippine National Bank.

Eugene started his leadership journey at a young age, first chairing his La Salle High School Student Council, and later at the University of San Carlos where he also led other student organizations. On the side, he majored in physics and graduated *magna cum laude*. He also completed the Advanced Management Program at Harvard Business School.

He recently wrote the novel *Never Stand Alone*, and posts regularly on LinkedIn where he was awarded top community voice badges in the areas of leadership, strategy, and management.

Francis and EJ Acevedo, at London School of Economics.

For EJ,

with love from Dad

I hope this book will be your guide

whenever I am far away.

Prologue

Who did I write this book for?

I wrote this book for my 20-year-old self, but I obviously cannot go back in time. What I wish I knew back then, they are all here. The chapters distill the wisdom I gathered in the last 40 years since I left university.

If I could mentor my young self, the words in the book are exactly what I would say. They are the same advice I shared with the over 100 young professionals during my stay at Citi, RCBC, PNB, and Unionbank, and the almost 40 mentees I meet on a regular basis.

If you have just started working, this book is for you. Actually, even the mid-careers will benefit from the discussions on leadership, strategy, and digital transformation.

Reading this book, you will know to prepare for professional advancement, how to make a good impression on recruiters, what skills to acquire early, how to dress the part, and even how to find a mentor.

Those who are in management will learn the finer points of leadership, and how to articulate a compelling strategy while building resilience. It is also critical that they turn their teams into outperformers.

The new environment demands that leaders understand and embrace digital and data science tools, particularly how to bolster the organization's transformation agenda. While these technical skills are now a prerequisite, soft skills are even more critical.

The last part will remind you to find balance. Work should not consume you; you need to become more than the work you do. Find trusting relationships with friends and colleagues, and affection from family and pets.

Finally, as my sons are now in their 20s and starting their careers halfway across the globe, this book will take the place of Dad talking. Thankfully it is just on paper, and without drama.

Introduction

I was first trained as a leader at the University of San Carlos, then at the Asian Institute of Management (AIM). After leaving school, I was mentored throughout my time at Citibank. Moving from one school to the next, and then to a boarding house near Citi, I carried a yellow duffel bag that contained all my belongings.

From those formative years until now, classroom training and mentoring continue to be the only ways I know how to build leaders. They also give me both personal and professional satisfaction.

I have been doing much writing over the last eight months on topics covering leadership, strategy, career development, mentorship, and digital banking. It started during long weekends in October 2023. Then I found myself typing in airports — Manila, Gatwick, Heathrow, Changi, Narita, Davao, Cebu and a few small ones far, far away across the globe in Barbados and Grenada. The longest single non-stop marathon was in Kathmandu.

Writing has become like a morning crossword puzzle to me. I will run out of topics at some point, I often said. But days after, I am typing away again.

This book contains my musings on LinkedIn. As of June 2024, I must have written over 200 posts. What I did was group similar articles into four parts, and later realized I could further subdivide them into chapters.

I hope you enjoy reading this book. It has been fulfilling writing all the pieces so far, and I still can't believe I have the audacity to actually write this second book. My advice is that you read a few pages each time. Don't binge. Savor the paragraphs, read between the lines, and find my hidden jokes.

This book wouldn't have been possible without the support of my senior leadership team at RCBC and the Office of the President. Much of what I have learned and written about was tested and practiced in our offices.

Finally, I am indebted to my Chairperson, Mrs. Helen Yuchengco Dee, for taking a risk on me, for sharing her wisdom, and for granting me a corner of the sky where I can try to be a better leader.

Table of Contents

Part One

Reinvent Yourself and Your Career

”

Leadership makes the results exponential.

Chapter One

Countdown to Launch

Lao Tzu once said, "The journey of a thousand miles begins with a single step."

I have quoted this wise piece of advice since high school. But, as a senior banker, I respectfully suggested a small addition: "… in the right direction." A first step in the wrong direction can set you farther from your goals. One may argue that the journey itself can be worth the experience acquired, even if it takes longer. That is well and good if the young person has ample time and resources.

While I write from a manager's point of view, this first set of articles hopes to set your aim closer to your target.

She Wants to Be a CEO

I no longer get shocked when approached by young professionals asking for my advice on how to be the CEO of a large company. They have been exposed to many leaders, and naturally, they aspire to reach the top job at some points in their careers.

This is what I say:

1. Be an expert in at least three disciplines, of which one should be sales. Being in sales improves the ability to be persuasive and builds empathy.

2. Keep studying, keep learning about new trends such as data, AI, and digitization, and read about leaders who did well in your industry.

3. Outperform your peers but do not be disagreeable. Volunteer for difficult tasks, particularly those that involve collaboration with other groups.

4. Take care of your health, exercise, and sleep well. Your body needs to withstand stress and still perform.

5. Diversify your sources of happiness: family, pets, friends, etc. You will need them during times of difficulty.

All these will improve your chances of getting to higher positions. But being a CEO, well, is also dependent on luck, on jobs opening up. For instance, there are years when no banks look for a new CEO.

Finally, don't announce your grand objective. Outwork your peers without calling attention to yourself.

I understand that diligence can also be noticed, but at least it is not the same as trumpeting your goals, which many can find annoying.

Are You a Triple Threat?

In showbiz, celebrities need to act, sing, and dance (in descending order of importance). Triple threats get more opportunities and career breaks.

I often compare this to banking, and urge young people to be skilled in at least three of these functional areas:

Operations and Controls
Sales and Relationship Management
Corporate Lending
Consumer Lending/Cards
Retail Banking
Trading and Balance Sheet Management
Digital Banking and Payments
Technology

Traditional companies, in general, tend to promote high-potential officers up a single vertical, mostly because siloed managers want to selfishly keep their talents for themselves. Thankfully companies now tend to move their top talent across several verticals to master new skills.

These multi-skilled high-potential individuals often end up as the company's future leaders.

Locally, I have seen a technology leader taking over as the CEO of an insurance company. This should inspire young professionals to ask for cross-posting early in their careers.

As a newbie in operations who transferred to trading, and later advanced to treasury sales, I benefited immensely from hands-on training before exiting Citi. Then I led retail and corporate lending functions at local banks, giving me a well-rounded resume. My story is not unique, but I hope that it becomes more common.

The wonderful side benefit of cross-posting is a wider network of friends and collaborators, even if the main objective is seasoning and preparation.

The Interview Never Stops

I have this technique when conducting interviews where I cut my time into slices of roughly 10 to 20 minutes. In the first slice, I check for soft skills. In the next, I assess competence. In the third, I sell the company and the job.

It used to matter much how the candidate walks in, how confident the handshake is, the grooming, the body language. These carry less weight to me now as our company also hires non-traditional bankers. The first few questions asked are meant to put him or her at ease. These questions are easy as they are about the candidate. What is more important is how they answer.

Then comes the competence part. I assess the person's value to the organization using what I call "performance math." It is individual skills multiplied by hard work, and again multiplied by the person's ability to work with other people. Leadership makes the results exponential.

Performance = (Individual skills x Hard work x Teamwork)^Leadership

Apart from grades and skills, I look for evidence of problem-solving, demonstrating ability to work well with people, and proven achievements in leadership positions.

One shortcut which my former employer used as a guide is to ask myself, "Do I see myself promoting this person to vice president in the future?" I still use this when I meet management trainees and other juniors, even when they are already working in the bank.

What young people need to realize is that the process never stops. Any interaction with a senior, particularly the ones who are keen on talent management, is an interview.

Continuing to the last part, when an interviewer starts describing to you how great the company is, it is a good indicator. I do this when I like the candidate. I don't waste time to make a sale.

Grade Conscious

I just read a newspaper column that discussed the perils of attention to grades over actual learning. I can't help but write my thoughts.

Ever since grade school, I have always put more emphasis on the joy of learning, hence I ventured beyond what the teachers gave us and read books on other topics. The same happened in college where I tried to split my time into three segments: learning, academics, and leadership.

I could have focused on academics, or academics and leadership together, and showed more exemplary grades. But that wasn't fun. No joy.

To be fair to my university, they actually encouraged personal development and awarded the Ten Outstanding Graduate (TOG) trophy to those who made the cut.

In graduate school, I worked part-time and studied really hard because I started with zero knowledge compared to classmates who had business backgrounds. Grades became a barometer of whether I learned enough to prepare myself for work after graduation.

All these affect how I hire. I look for balance. I look for curiosity, for leadership, for proof of EQ and influence skills. Of course I look at grades as well because, if the candidate can have a balanced college life while attaining Latin honors, then he/she is worthy of consideration. To some extent, grades demonstrate diligence. Hard work.

Nowadays, when everyone graduates from kindergarten with a medal, and when Latin honors are more common, it is harder to discern. Assessing leadership is doubly difficult because student organizations have notoriously created a gazillion positions copying corporations. I have to ask exactly what they did as assistant vice president for whatever.

But I will never ignore grades. They are important, but there are at least two others that carry similar or even more weight.

Prepare for a New Job

There are books on what you need to do when entering a new organization. I confess I never read them.

However, there was always a formula I followed in the eight times I joined a new company or moved to a new country.

These were what I did BEFORE the first day of work:

1. Learned much about the business I was taking over. Annual reports and news articles were useful. Google as well. Noted down important financial numbers. Mystery shopped when appropriate, visited their facilities, and saw how they served customers.

2. Got to know the main personalities. (This is now easier because of LinkedIn, Facebook, and mutual friends.) Found similarities with new colleagues, had a plan to build relationships. Memorized faces and names.

3. Drafted a transformation plan on how the business will be able to significantly improve its financials. This was later refined when actually on site.

Then there was the matter of personal logistics. It became way more complicated when I moved to a new country. It opened up a new set of issues: children's school, place to live, travel documents, pets, and so on. The first thing I did was call my friends who made a similar move.

The idea is to reduce the level of uncertainty and stress early on. You will be absorbing a ton of information soon, so better start getting them early.

Don't just hit the ground running. Run before you start. Be in the zone.

Building Sales Careers

I have always found that hiring those with some sales experience, and then teaching them banking, has a maximum 50% chance of success. It is costly, but still better than hiring those without sales skills.

Recruiting salespeople from other banks has a higher success ratio, but is way more expensive.

My preference has always been to promote from within. Tellers become new accounts clerks, and then become accustomed to dealing directly with customers. This new behavior, coupled with training, can lead to a successful career in sales.

This same practice extends to other parts of the bank. Marketing assistants in wealth and corporate banking can become outstanding senior bankers. Same in consumer loans and small and medium enterprises. Most of our sales directors started from entry-level positions in branches. Their career stories are inspiring.

The analogy holds true for other companies.

This is why I insist on hiring with future roles in mind, not just the current one. What I mean is, while assessing an assistant, check their potential for senior jobs. This is quite like the "will this person make it to vice president" question. This time it will be, "Can this young lady run a branch in 10 years?"

This internal preference also has to do with motivation. Sure, we give incentives for performance beyond targets. But I find that having productive career growth is a stronger, longer-term reason for staying and performing.

When employees start calling the company their second home, or their second family, it starts to feel more than just loyalty. It is love.

A Salesperson's Job Isn't Easy

I often watch elegantly dressed young people handing out flyers of a real estate company. Their booth is right in front of the mall driveway, near a Japanese restaurant.

Thousands of pedestrians cross the area every day. It is like a river filled with salmon. And the salespersons are watching the current, ready to pounce.

They don't approach every person. They choose. What is their basis? I try to avoid their gaze, looking down, but they often call me even if I am in shorts and sandals. When caught, I say that I already have an account officer.

Even if I try to ignore them, they insist on giving me marketing material "for reference."

Whenever I have a meal at the Japanese restaurant, I watch them like they are an experiment in human behavior. Some people obviously avoid them (those are the targets). I feel sad when they have no meaningful contact, or even a brief conversation, with anyone in an hour. I quietly cheer them on. Every hour, a new batch of five salespeople take their place.

Naturally, to satisfy my curiosity, I asked one of their company seniors, whom I had lunch with, why they stood patiently under the sun. Was it worth the effort?

It turns out that the spot is one of their best. Salespeople actually wait for their turn to be based here. To use my oft-repeated phrase, this is like "fishing from a fishpond!" Now, I don't feel sad for them anymore.

Perhaps I should reverse roles and ask them if they want to join the bank.

Sales and Political Science

I cannot ignore the correlation — there are simply too many successful sales leaders who were political science and legal management majors in college. I see them in banking, in technology, companies selling services, in start-ups, and in product management.

These individuals probably initially wanted to be lawyers, but later changed their minds and joined the workforce instead of suffering through thousands of court cases.

But why are they successful as sales leaders? Let me try to describe them.

1. They can talk. They have better communication skills than most other majors, which helps when selling and leading.

2. They reason well, can anticipate what the other person might say, and find a way to persuade and close a sale.

3. They don't necessarily take a disapproval personally and can move on to another discussion.

4. Research skills enable them to understand the client better.

5. A number of them are charmers.

Whenever I see a political science major, I am generally inclined to hire them. Based on the comments I read on LinkedIn, many of my connections turned out to be political science majors who became sales leaders. Now I have even more proof of my theory!

Which brings me to a related point — if this theory is believable, why then don't we have many lawyers doing sales?

Talk to Yourself

When you want to be promoted, talk to yourself first, quietly.

Ask yourself, have you really outperformed others to have the right to move ahead? Is your KRA (Key Result Areas) score consistently higher? One good year may not be enough. In some organizations, performance rankings are transparent, or at least production is clearly comparable.

Are you hoping because you have stayed long enough? Tenure is good, but way less important than performance. The best combination is performance and tenure together.

Have you done anything outstanding that added significant value to the company? Is your position rated correctly for the rank you are aspiring for, or are you hoping management will make an exception?

If you don't have clear answers to the questions, then that is the first problem. You need to know where you stand.

Talk to your boss and HR first. But be ready to hear a frank response. Best to get the facts because now you will know how you can do better.

I am sure you will want to seek sympathy from friends who will generally agree with you and make the matter worse. Pick the right friend to consult. Do you have someone close who can be brutally honest with you? A mentor, perhaps.

Don't worry, not being promoted is not the end of your career. It "builds character!" In the future, I expect some of these sad episodes will be a good source of anecdotes. Finally, once you know what you need to do to be worthy, make a go for it.

When I Was Not Promoted, Three Times

Over four days, through various customer, regulatory, and board meetings, I got to sit beside a fellow bank CEO. We always compared notes, and one of the topics we talked about was how important social media was in our jobs. I complimented him on his recent post about getting passed over for a promotion three times in his career. His post made me recall my own list of three.

My first miss was my promotion to assistant vice president (AVP). Because the bank had losses during the US real estate crisis, the country head unilaterally decided, on the morning of the announcement, to delay officer promotions by six months. I was devastated.

Second, my promotion to VP which I got on time. Unfortunately, a year later, I found out exactly what happened. The country promotion board disapproved it based on a technicality, but regional treasury management insisted and got their way. As a result, I had mixed feelings and felt inadequate.

In both instances, I turned negative emotions into an "I will show you I deserve it" attitude, which provided constructive momentum for the next promotion (the SVP equivalent) that came without any drama.

The third was when I was told, over dinner, that I was not getting the top job. I must say that the manner of delivery was done very well. I had too many glasses of (very expensive) red wine that I had trouble standing up after three hours. It became a joke later between the holding company chairman and me that I had emptied his cellar. It is for this reason that, until now, I continue to have immense respect for the late chairman and his cousin. Still, I had clear feelings about it, and changed my career plans as a result.

Missing a promotion is an emotional experience that is hard to forget, especially if you have the numbers to back it up. It also matters how the bad news is delivered.

”

Real men wear pink and we’re all for it.

Chapter Two

Look Like You Made It

I feel a little guilty that I do not have articles in this chapter to assist women, but I really have no expertise in that department. However, it quickly became obvious that my posts on how the male gender should dress up were more popular among women; they forwarded them to their partners.

This reminds me of a husband who went to Victoria's Secret with his wife. After browsing the displays, he impatiently asked the saleslady, "Do you have anything here for men?" She responded firmly, "Sir, everything we have here is for men!"

Brown Shoes and Style 101 for Young Men

In my early years as a senior banker, I noticed that young men in the bank needed some guidance on dressing up. I often saw them wearing orange or red shirts with black ties, and black shirts with silver ties.

I recalled the time when I was clueless, and took it upon myself to write this guide:

1. If you want to play it safe, wear light-colored plain shirts in white, pink, and blue. Try white collars and cuffs. Other shirt colors (orange, red, etc.) are tricky.

2. Ties should generally have a darker shade than the shirt. Put a dimple on your tie knot. Avoid the black or gray shirt with light tie combo unless you moonlight for a steak restaurant or a band.

3. Striped ties are better with plain shirts. But if you feel bold and want to wear a striped shirt, the tie stripes should be wider than the shirt stripes. And they should share a similar color.

4. If you are wearing a bold shirt, like a checkered one, wear a plain, sober tie.

5. Wear dark socks that match your pants. If you feel adventurous and want to wear colored socks, do not wear a patterned shirt or striped suit. They will clash.

6. The belt should match your shoes. Don't use a brown belt with black shoes. Better yet, don't wear a belt at all, like Korean actors. I usually don't.

7. Wear brown, tan, or burgundy shoes only with pale or navy blue suits. For suits in midnight blue and dark gray, pick dark chocolate brown shoes. Never wear brown shoes with black or near-black suits.

8. The coat and pants should match unless you are wearing a blazer or sports coat (more business casual). If you wear a blue blazer, wear gray or khaki pants, never blue or black. Contrast is key.

9. The tie should reach the upper part of the belt and not go lower.

10. Leave the lower coat button unbuttoned. Do not button everything. Only JFK and little boys are exempted from this rule.

11. Show some shirt sleeve, about half an inch, when wearing a coat. If more than an inch shows, have the shirt altered.

12. Slim cut is preferred, and flat front without pleats. Pants should not be too long, with only one break (wrinkle) and not much cloth hanging around the shoes.

13. Finally, if your suit is new, cut the threads from the pocket openings and the vents. You can't imagine how many times I had to cut the vent threads from new suits of younger bankers. Have it dry-cleaned, especially if the tailor's chalk marks are showing. One lady CEO still reminds me of the time I pointed out the chalk marks in her blazer. She was just new in the bank then.

When having your first suit made, pick navy blue. Next, medium gray. They match most shirts. Then black for special events. Do pinstripes later. Your original navy blue jacket can be repurposed into a blazer when the pants get old or worn out.

Find a good tailor and make him your friend for life. My shirtmaker has done work for my father, brothers, sons, and nephews. But my suit cutter recently retired and migrated to Canada.

Men's Shoes All Look the Same (or Your Guide to Shoe Taxonomy)

Do you struggle to tell the difference between men's shoes? Even though I can distinguish between Oxfords, Derbies, Single Monks, Double Monks, Brogues, Wingtips, Cap-toes, Tassels, Loafers, and even Tux shoes, my wife still claims they all look the same!

For those who are unfamiliar:

Oxfords are plain, closed lace-ups, while Derbies are open lace-ups.

Single Monks have one buckle on the side, while Double Monks have two.

Brogues have designs made using tiny holes, either fully-brogued or partial if just in front.

Wing-tips have a front cover that extends to the sides like wings, although some extend to the heel.

Cap-toes have a cap sewn on the front part, while Tassels are self-explanatory.

Loafers are a more casual cut, and Tux shoes are in a simple Oxford lace-up design typically in patent leather.

But wait, it gets even more complicated. In the office, brogued Wingtips are popular, but I prefer Oxford cap-toes without brogues as they are easier to mirror shine. And for a classy look, plain Single Monks are my go-to. I rotate these three every week. But if you're feeling bold, Double Monk Wingtips are the way to go.

My personal favorite is a pair of burgundy Oxfords with a bit of brogue and a medallion or design on the toe. What's your favorite style of men's shoes?

Mirror Shoe Shine Therapy

During long weekends, I force the serious half of my brain to shut off. The best distraction is taking care of my shoes, most of which have been with me for nearly a decade. I should actually give them names. Most men would do the normal routine of a single coat of wax, then brush all over. To be fair, that is often good enough. But for me it isn't.

I prefer to mirror shine my shoes using shoe wax, cold water, and a soft cloth. Yes, water!

There are irrational methods in shoe shining. Apart from water, use black shoe polish on brown shoes. Yes, black! I learned this from men's magazines. Black polish leaves a rustic look on the toe and in the seams.

This makes for a perfect therapeutic activity. Apply six layers of wax on areas that need extra shining but do not fold (the creases), like the front tip. After 10 minutes, wet a piece of cloth slightly with cold water and gently rub on the surface. Apply a bit more wax. Gently rub with wet cloth. Use a light touch.

Repeat until you are satisfied with the result. Finish off gently with soft cotton. Old T-shirts with holes are preferred.

Okay, let me explain. What happens is that layers of wax build up a smooth film on top of the leather surface, just like a mirror.

This will take some practice, but eventually you will get the hang of it.

The downside of this article is that my male friends keep checking out my shoes when I meet them. The only friends who are unimpressed are those raised in military families. As boys, they copied the spit-and-shine their fathers did.

Real Men Wear Pink

In the early '90s, your friend here had a pink shirt, an oxford with a white collar. But when he wore it to the Hong Kong Trading Room, he was met with stares and even a point-blank question from a female colleague about his choice of color.

No other man on the floor wore pink; it was all white or blue.

But the next day, four male colleagues surprisingly wore pink shirts. And soon after, it became a usual thing. They just needed someone to start the trend.

Pink is not the easiest color to match. It pairs well with ties in certain (not all) shades of green, blue, and maroon. The most fashion-forward guy I know paired it with a shade of mustard (the tie, not the sauce). Bold and elegant.

Since pink is bound to attract more attention, it's best to iron the shirt well, especially the chest part which shows when wearing a suit. The secret? Spray starch! And the suit is best navy blue, at least in the business setting.

If you check research, the color pink calms people down. It does have an effect. I often wear a pink tie or a pink shirt (but not together!) when making a difficult presentation.

As for other colors, I hesitate to experiment. I have some in pale purple, even in purple stripes. And light green. These are all easy to match ties with.

It just goes to show that sometimes all it takes is one person to step out of the norm and inspire others to do the same. Real men wear pink and we're all for it!

Office Uniform

As a banker, my office uniform is a crucial part of my daily routine. While I may not be able to wear the same outfit every day like Zuckerberg does, I've found a formula that works for me.

My go-to outfit consists of a white shirt with plain cuffs, a blue suit, and black shoes that follow a rotation. The tie is where I get to have a little fun. If I'm meeting with a client, I'll wear their company color. If it's a special occasion, like Valentine's Day or New Year's, I'll opt for red. For bank events, light blue or green is my go-to. And if I'm presenting, I might opt for a pink tie. Celebrations call for yellow, red, or orange.

I rarely use French cuffs nowadays; they take longer to put on. My cufflinks only come out of the drawers for tuxedos.

When it comes to tie width, I follow a simple rule. If I'm wearing a single-breasted suit, I pick a slim tie. If it's double-breasted, a regular-width tie matches the dimensions better.

As for suits, I wear single-breasted ones most days. The doubles are for occasions which are a bit special. You might ask me when the doubles made a comeback. The answer: Korean dramas.

On days when I don't wear a tie, I'll opt for a striped or plaid shirt, or even pink. I avoid white shirts on these days as I would look too plain. Then a pocket square completes the outfit and replaces the tie as an accent piece.

The general idea is not to spend much time thinking about what to wear, as my mind quickly shifts into work mode in the mornings. I can't do what one of my colleagues used to fix every weekend. He would organize which suits, shirts, and ties to wear for the week ahead. He is Italian.

What's your go-to office uniform?

Colorful Socks

When my previous bank decided to go all-out digital, even with outfits, I stocked up on colored socks. The collection grew exponentially as my colleagues decided socks would be my default birthday and Christmas gifts. I even received half a dozen black-and-whites.

Try the Happy brand. If you transit in Dubai or are in IFC Mall in Hong Kong, look for the shop that sells Paul Smith striped socks in various colors.

How to wear them:

1. Put them on but pretend they don't exist. Ignore them. If you keep checking them out, you are not worthy.
2. Don't match with loud and patterned blazers and shirts. Best to wear plain uppers.
3. Avoid pocket squares unless they are plain.
4. If you are wearing them with a suit, opt for plain suits and choose simpler sock patterns like stripes from Paul Smith. Or argyles which are classy. Not designs of hamburgers or mugs of beer.
5. Try to stay in a similar shade as your pants or shoes so as not to draw attention.
6. Try to manage a small gap between your pants and shoes. Don't wear pants that are too long.
7. Wear socks with hearts during weddings or on Valentine's. Use socks to celebrate events.

The most important rule: Your socks should match your personality and performance. Your work should be remarkable, innovative, or fun.

If you are behind budget, stick with black socks.

Why Wear a Tux

The tuxedo or dinner jacket is appropriate for the most formal evening events. For bankers, that means awards ceremonies, weddings, and gala affairs.

It is typically in black, or even in ivory (my preferred alternate color), although I've read that the original tux was in very dark blue. The black or blue jacket has black satin lapels and buttons.

Ivory lapels, on the other hand, look more elegant if made from the same fabric as the jacket. Not satin. I credit *Casablanca* for this observation.

This brings me to Humphrey Bogart's style of wearing a double-breasted tuxedo, instead of the usual single-breasted. If you can pull it off, go for it.

There are rules on wearing them, including using a tuxedo shirt with wingtip collar, a cummerbund around the waist, French cuffs with simple silver cufflinks, a black silk bow tie, very shiny plain lace-up shoes, no belt, and black trousers with a satin stripe along the side seams.

There are those who wear jackets that are made of heavy curtain-like materials in striking colors. They look great when holding a trophy. Bravo to them.

For those just starting out, you can put together a black bow tie, a neatly pressed plain white shirt, a regular black suit, black socks, and well-shined, plain, lace-up shoes. Don't deviate. In a large evening crowd, most people will not notice the minor details, especially if you have a warm, charming smile.

Since you seldom wear your tux, you should have them dry-cleaned and stored well. The real challenge though, is fitting into them after many years.

”

Imperfection is often a source of inspiration or strength.

Chapter Three

Softly as I Lead You

Some call it EQ (emotional quotient). I prefer to use the more general term — soft skills, which refer to communication and social skills, self-management, and more.

Soft skills are portable. They are useful regardless of the type of work or position. The only problem is that you don't necessarily acquire them by sitting in school. Soft skills are learned through experience.

As you go up the ladder, soft skills carry more consequence.

If You Are Brilliant, Why Aren't You Rich?

This condescending comment comes in many combinations. Articles are even written about valedictorians who struggle after graduation. Yes, even after nerds started leading the list of billionaires. I honestly found this annoying as this became an excuse for academic non-performance.

I am obviously biased, being a valedictorian myself. In graduate school, a classmate even told me that the real test is who gets to be a CEO.

The first argument against this is that, in the new economy where quantitative and technical skills are more sought after, the pay scales have favored the nerds.

The second point is that many intelligent people find more excitement in the pursuit of knowledge, or in their passion to serve others. That is their definition of wealth.

Not everyone is focused on material objects. Clearly you need a certain level of comfort, but Maslow's hierarchy tells us that physiological needs lay at the bottom of the pyramid. Once those are satisfied, humans look for safety, love, self-esteem, and so on.

Years from now, when I am sitting on some comfortable chair somewhere, I will be thinking of my investments. Not financial. In people! In the more than 100 mentees I had under my care over the last two decades in the five banks I served in.

I will feel much more gratification knowing that the ones I chose have done well in life, and I had the opportunity to start them right, influence them midway, and take care of them throughout their journey.

That is my wealth.

Lesson from *Love Actually*

I watched the movie many times during long flights. It is not boring as it has multiple storylines. However, when I don't have much time left, I go to my favorite part which has to do with the miserable British author and his shy Portuguese housekeeper. These characters are played by Colin Firth and Lúcia Moniz.

If you remember their story, the author rented a cottage where he could do his writing. I don't recall whether it was a romance or mystery novel. The landlady arranged for a housekeeper to help him with his needs. As bad luck would have it, the young lady did not understand English (which did not sit well with me knowing how the two countries were allied against Napoleon and Spain, and are united in their love for a glass of port).

They couldn't speak each other's language, yet managed to communicate through the cutest nonverbals until the author's manuscript was completed. Nothing significant happened despite the obvious attraction.

We often hear that nonverbals make up 90% of communication. The way you look at the other person, the tone of voice, your body language, and more. But the movie suggests that nonverbals may still be incomplete. Words in the appropriate language are needed to close the deal, as depicted in the movie when the author learned broken Portuguese and the lady understood some English.

I am reminded of the Bee Gees' song *Words*, and how words can be powerful.

I overanalyze. It is a slow day in the office.

Gut Feel

I read somewhere that feeling and thinking are essentially the same, except that feeling is the brain in hyperdrive, while thinking is slower. Much, much slower. When something does not seem right, there is a good chance you are correct.

During interviews, although not frequently, I sometimes get an odd feeling. I usually ask HR to do more homework. More often than not, I get negative feedback.

As a trader, I read market updates and analysis every day. But during actual market hours, or when I worked on a deal, it felt like my body went on autopilot. Over two decades of treasury work must have done that.

My most significant trading decisions started with my stomach feeling weird (before selling equities in 2008, for example) or feeling euphoric immediately before loading up on bonds a couple of years ago. Somehow, all the information accumulated over time triggered some buy or sell signals.

The most interesting explanation I found was that this was the four F limbic system at work. Fight or flight. Then the need for feeding. And finally, fulfilling the desire for reproduction.

What do I do next? I used to act on it immediately. Now, I treat it as a warning. Since I have the ability to source information quickly, I spend the next few minutes confirming my gut feeling.

(Later, in another section, we will take one step further and confirm gut feel with data analytics. Thankfully, with faster computing power and advanced skills, making decisions based on data is now easier and more convenient.)

Time is More Than Money

Young people don't know this, but we used to pay airport fees a long, long time ago. Now we generally don't (or are charged less), but we have to walk more than three times as long past shops and restaurants as airports have become malls.

The same goes for train stations like those in Hong Kong. Commercial establishments jockey for spaces which are levied high rent.

When I don't pay at all, while enjoying some benefit, I am the product. Like poultry that eat twice a day and realize, belatedly, that they are the product. The shops and restaurants in airports and train stations are the customers. They "consume" us, sort of.

At least the exercise adds to my 10,000 daily steps. I don't complain as it seems like a good bargain.

What if I don't want to waste time, like in traffic? How do you flip this argument? Singapore did. I want the convenience of having my own car with manageable traffic? Pay SGD 77,000 for the COE (certificate of entitlement, which is the right to buy a car, in addition to the price of the car itself!). It works only when public transport is efficient. In many Asian cities, paying for a driver allows one to work during the time otherwise lost in traffic.

There are indeed many ways to think about the value of time.

Ten years ago, we discussed in class the value of athlete brands during the athlete's lifetime. Time value builds up as one gets to his/her peak productivity, and slopes down as one approaches their twilight years.

Time is money, but more, because it allows you to gain memories that you can't put a price on.

Complete the Story

When I read the news, it does not take long to scan the headlines and the first paragraphs. This is because news is meant to be brief. I remember being told as a young editor that the who, what, when, where, and how have to be described at the start, and the details can follow in order of decreasing importance — the inverted pyramid. That way, the person in charge of layout can cut paragraphs away to fit all the pieces together on a page.

The problem with this is that news becomes less interesting and impersonal. It has gotten boring. We now hardly finish an article because it is essentially summarized at the start.

I prefer the style of *Time* magazine which almost always tells the story from a personal point of view, often with rich descriptions of the territory, while painting a picture of the protagonist. Even esoteric concepts like quantum physics discoveries become readable for the uninitiated. And we read until the end.

The recently launched local news start-ups follow this formula. That explains their growing readership and interest. It is easier to relate to a person than to a concept.

Over time, I have learned to compensate. It is not enough to read the news. I google the personalities and the places involved; otherwise, I miss the context of the story. Its history.

Even when listening to a speaker for the first time, especially if the topic is quite interesting, I google their background or check LinkedIn.

News can't simply be about facts; it should tell a story. The same goes for your next business presentation. Otherwise, you will lose your audience at the start.

Powerless Point

It is hard to get used to people using PowerPoint presentations as a way to display their word files. It is an exercise in patience. Paragraphs upon paragraphs torture me. I can read faster than they can read their own stuff.

Or, the slide is busy. And they start by apologizing for the cluttered slide.

There are exceptions.

I have learned a few tricks over decades of presenting:

1. Place the slide titles at the upper left corner, exactly in the same spot on each slide. The slide titles, when read one after another, should summarize the entire presentation. The human eye is trained to start reading from the upper left.

2. Use the fewest words possible. Try to delete words and sentences so the font size is bigger. The presentation is a guide to your talk. Don't read.

3. Limit each slide to six objects only, with a group of short lines counting as one object. (I learned this in a UX certification course.)

4. Avoid using 1,000% in tables, with rare exceptions, as they usually mean you are just starting the project/product and the numbers are still small. I call this the law of small numbers.

5. The right charts can convey the message better and faster than words or tables. Make sure they do not mislead.

In the end, this usually is a matter of personal style. And the final test is whether the audience is looking at you rather than the slides.

It's Only Words

Actually, it is not. In conversations and when writing, the choice of words and the way the sentence is structured can change the message. When speaking, the tone and body language matters.

Nowadays, the font size, capitalization, and context complicate the process in social media. All caps mean someone is yelling.

But what I would really want to stress is the choice of words. I remember being told in high school to use a fancy word every week to help build vocabulary. And our parish priest would use a heavy word up to three times in every Sunday sermon. Mass enriched us both spiritually and linguistically. That was the case until my father and his best friend decided that the sermon was the best time to have a cigarette.

In fact, there is a columnist who publishes very well-analyzed articles but peppers them with elite-sounding words. I stopped checking his corner even if I knew what the fancy words meant. I got the feeling that his writing was meant to impress, rather than communicate.

The former dean of Harvard Business School, Nitin Nohria, wrote insightful pieces which are informative and persuasive, without the need to check the dictionary. Writing simply, simply works.

I have to add that writing love notes is in a special class by itself. Oh, the sweetness of youth and innocence distilled into a few lines.

I prefer words we use in daily conversations, and to write as I speak. Finally, I would rather put humor and play into sentence structure, as that makes the piece entertaining.

And yes, when written well, words can take your heart away.

When People Pull You Down

Crab mentality is a disease that consumes some, and seems to convince them that they elevate themselves when they pull other people down with malicious or even harmless remarks. They cannot be happy for the successes of others. They always need to point out what is imperfect, not realizing that the imperfection is often a source of inspiration or strength.

What the crabs fail to realize is that those around them simply tolerate them or actually hold them in lower regard, and are cautious when they are present because they are toxic.

What to do with crabs? Unlike the ones in East Coast that are best with black pepper, or with butter and garlic, these crabs are better avoided. Don't waste your time with them. Don't give them an audience. Ignore them.

Or if you can tolerate them, treat them as if you had no idea they have been bashing you. Keep them wondering. Be friendly.

Surround yourself instead with friends who support you. Those who will give you constructive criticism. Friends who will pull you aside when you make a mistake because they want you to be a better person. Friends who will protect you.

I found these allies as early as elementary school, and through the years, especially during bad times.

You may not be able to choose your relatives or your officemates, but you can choose your friends.

When you find good ones, treasure them.

When You Say Nothing at All

Many board meetings ago, after a long discussion on a controversial topic, our most senior director turned to me because he couldn't remember the quote that meant silence was better. I knew he was looking for one of those old Confucian type sayings, but instead I chose Ronan Keating's song from the movie *Notting Hill*. He smiled when I quickly replied, "When you say nothing at all."

Silence can be powerful in appropriate occasions.

"Pregnant pauses" while looking at the crowd can punctuate key emotional or declarative statements. It gives people time to think, to absorb, to feel.

A short silence after hearing a disagreeable comment allows you to process and understand the other party's point of view. He/she realizes that you probably aren't enthusiastic, but are civil. I remember having a staring contest during a meeting after a visitor spoke, as I was unwilling to engage on the topic just raised. It must have lasted for five minutes.

You use the time to choose your words, unless you prefer not to speak. Not immediately responding may also give a signal that it requires more thinking, or is probably not readily acceptable.

This is no different from not making hasty decisions when emotional. The decision might probably still be the same afterwards, but the delivery is more calibrated

There are, of course, situations where silence is inappropriate. That topic is for another day. Otherwise, when the context calls for diplomacy, best to remember that you cannot take back a spoken word. Best to be firm but polite, to disagree but not be disagreeable.

The Unkindest Cut of All

Sometimes, in my mentoring sessions, I am asked about interpersonal relationships, collaboration, and loyalty. This is when I quote the "unkindest cut." This phrase comes from William Shakespeare's *Julius Caesar*, where the latter was betrayed and stabbed by his friend Brutus.

Nowadays, it means that the most painful of rumors, slights, and abuse come from people you thought were your close friends, and you expected some decent degree of reciprocal loyalty from them.

Life seems double-edged. The higher you go, the less anonymous you become, the more adverse treatment you get. Oftentimes, people just feel the need to say something bad to be viewed as being in the know, while not really intending malice.

Part of the problem is that some of these comments eventually reach you. The more loyal friends you have, the more likely. What to do? Don't allow them to lurk rent-free in your head. Continue to be civil. After all, it comes with the territory. The upside is that you discover who your real friends are.

What happens then when you have the opportunity to get back at your detractors? Tempting, isn't it? I have realized that it isn't worth it. I don't get any pleasure from it at all. There will probably be exceptions, but I have not found them yet, thankfully.

In the meantime, I remind myself that doing well is the best revenge, even if it really isn't.

Remember, only when you have detractors will you truly know that you matter. Call it free publicity.

Intellectual Modesty and Best Ideas

One of the traits I look for in my senior leaders is intellectual modesty. I define this as a healthy level of curiosity, drive for perpetual learning, the willingness to seek the opinion of others, respect for different points of view, and the readiness to admit mistakes.

This type of leader, like good wine, gets better with age. They rise in value.

Modesty implies the presence of skill, of expertise, but it is not flaunted nor rubbed in the faces of everyone else.

The inverse of this is a know-it-all who thinks he/she is better than everyone else — an intellectual bully who may or may not be an intellectual after all. Oftentimes, it's just a front.

We once had a roommate in the dormitory who loved talking about everything he knew. I tolerated it for a few days until I noticed everyone was already annoyed. I challenged him to a trivia contest, and he lost miserably. He promptly moved out, and we celebrated for days.

Intellectual modesty is a glue that builds personal relationships and strong teamwork. It also tends to yield better ideas, as brainstorming sessions become spontaneous and creative. And enjoyable.

This does not mean that there are no opposing ideas. There will be. But they are delivered in a constructive manner, maybe even with banter.

A leader fosters the right behavior by encouraging teammates to contribute, and by appreciating opinions which may be very radically different from his own.

It is not that the best idea wins; oftentimes, what wins is a combination of ideas.

Confirmation Bias

I kept repeating the phrase "confirmation bias" to describe a document that I was reading. I thought it misled the audience because it was one-sided.

What I meant was that the writer chose and gave weight only to those pieces of information that supported his/her conclusion. Facts or pieces of evidence which were contrary were ignored or belittled. I sometimes call this "convenience sampling."

Nowadays, false news is "confirmed" if the next person thinks similarly. It is not the same as confirmation bias itself, though it highlights a departure from facts. It is actually worse.

What causes this? Many things. Perhaps the writer is hell-bent on making his point. Having no access to contrary data is different from not looking for contrary data. You cannot see what you deliberately ignore. Yes, it is deliberate.

In high school science, we looked for evidence that disproved theories. We agreed with the conclusion only if we could not refute it. Unfortunately, this is not how the real world works.

At my grad school in AIM, our professors encouraged dissenting opinions. Learning gets stunted when everyone stands on the same side. Facts and conclusions should be challenged, albeit politely. At Harvard, our professor decided to hold a formal debate.

As a leader, one needs to be cautious of this fallacy as it is prevalent. When someone uses this reasoning against you, you need to call out the erroneous logic. I must warn you that it is often not worth engaging. For the non-believer, no explanation is possible. For the believer, no explanation is necessary.

"I Don't Know"

I avoid saying that line as there are better ways to address things, but there are times when it has to be uttered.

For example, if I receive an email or text asking a question, I may go into overdrive on Google looking for the answer. Or I call people who might know. It helps that text messages give you some time before responding. Use it!

If I am asked face-to-face, I will honestly say I am not sure but might offer a possible answer or a person who would be an expert on the topic. Or I say "let's find out" and google right then and there.

When asked in a presentation, especially if the point raised is totally unexpected and potentially leading to new approaches and insights, I thank the person and explain that, even if I don't know the answer, I am also very interested to find out.

Obviously, before presenting, you overprepare. A former boss once famously declared, "Prepare for 100 questions." He subjected subordinates to the equivalent of an oral exam, so he meant it.

I have realized that it seems acceptable to say the line, but only if the respondent is familiar with your level of competence and diligence. After all, there are basic facts that we are expected to know. When used repeatedly, the line can affect our reputation adversely.

However, I know some brilliant people who use the line in a (annoyingly) charming way. I wish I can do the same! When asked, they look at the source in a pensive way and say "I don't know" in a manner that compliments. This is usually followed by a long treatise on what might be the answer and how to find out. Beloved professors do this.

Ignorance is the beginning of knowledge, but ignorance of basic expectations is the beginning of the end of your job.

On Investments

Last Christmas, I sat beside a retired CEO who is well-known for his expertise in management and engineering. He answered a ton of questions until we got into investments, when he shared that 90% of his assets are in real estate. I assumed he had little debt.

This was an eye-opener because most textbooks will teach that equities, over the long run, will beat fixed income. Real estate is for diversification and does not provide quick liquidity if you need cash for emergency purposes, although rent is useful as passive income.

In my home country, starting 1993, the equities market became popular. For some time now, unfortunately, it has been disappointing. Ten year bonds and time deposits at 6% have become more attractive for the time being. This has prompted local investors to diversify into foreign or global equities.

On the other hand, real estate prices in this country seem to have climbed for years, slept for a while, before going up again. Compared to what I saw in Singapore and Hong Kong (where my rent once doubled in a year), it has not been volatile. In Hong Kong, I moved out of a flat next to IFC Mall and crossed over to the Elements Mall neighborhood where the rent is cheaper.

What is consistent with western markets is that crises provide an opportunity to buy. I wouldn't say "blood in the streets," but every cycle pushes the prices low enough that buying equities becomes a rational bet.

Finally, on crypto. I once followed the price action for about half a year together with a team of fintech enthusiasts. It is really up to the investor, as he can play with a limited amount that he/she is willing to risk. The younger ones can afford to experiment.

”

You don’t choose your mentor. Your mentor chooses you.

Chapter Four

Find Your Jedi Master

The Star Wars franchise has inspired legions of mentors and apprentices, me included. Mentors are now sometimes affectionately called "Master!" Mentors are more than teachers, they are storytellers. Because of their wealth of experience, somehow most questions asked can be richly answered through real-life accounts.

You don't choose your mentor. Your mentor chooses you. They have that luxury. They pick the ones who have promise and are worthy of their time. Just like in the movies.

My Brilliant Cambridge Hire

One day in 2003, a bright, young Singaporean sat across from me. I was interviewing her for the second batch of management trainees we were going to hire for Citi Financial Markets.

She came with impeccable credentials — first-class honors when she took her bachelor's and master's in chemical engineering at Cambridge. (She later took art seriously and earned another master's degree in art history, while diving into start-ups. Now, she heads investment transformation at a leading Asian bank.)

We were looking for candidates with quantitative backgrounds as we were expanding the derivatives and options teams. Every single STEM resume was evaluated. This was before digital and data became attractive career options. Interestingly, there was a good supply of engineers who graduated from foreign schools, and the top two Singapore universities.

The interview went smoothly, and I even asked her if she had questions about the bank and the program. We were about to end when I recalled something in her resume.

Since I was unfamiliar with the grading system, I asked many questions, and she patiently explained in her husky voice. I was particularly curious about her topping the tripos exams, which sounded impressive. But I had to ask why it was called "tripos" as it seemed like a unique tradition.

She shared that the final exams at Cambridge used to be held in halls where students sat on three-legged chairs as the floors were then uneven.

Oh, I exclaimed. A stool exam!

This story will never die.

The Triangle Career Approach

When younger people, which now means anyone below 50 years old, ask me for advice, I usually give them the practical equivalent of what Steve Jobs said. Do something you are passionate about, but make sure you will be able to support your family comfortably.

However, I actually find that approach lacking in seriousness. After all, giving advice can significantly alter the lives of those who trust our opinions.

Over the years, what has worked for me has been the triangle approach. I first find out what the person really wants to do, but ask more questions to confirm that the answer is consistent with his/her actual activities. Second, I assess what he/she is good at — skills, achievements, and how he/she compares with peers. Finally, and this is where I can contribute some knowledge, I share what attractive career opportunities are available, and how to position him/her for future growth.

Once some conclusion is reached, I usually connect the person to the right contacts to be able to pursue the new dream, and plan how to further build their skills to exploit the identified opportunity.

Mentoring is not a one-time event. A couple of months later, I usually check in to ensure that he/she is making progress.

The last time this happened, I was sitting in the airport lounge when a young lady asked Uncle ESA (my initials) about data science. She was a management undergrad working in asset management. I, understandably, was concerned about her math preparation even if I knew their family math DNA was strong.

Happy to share that she self-learned heavy math, passed the entrance exams, and is now pursuing a master's degree in data science.

Why Get a Mentor?

The best part about having a mentor is that you learn from his/her stories, and these are entertaining and difficult to forget. There is a reason why, even without written records, tribes had tales handed over across generations. They have staying power and are passed on. The mentor's anecdotes, often unstructured, help the new manager adjust emotionally and intellectually.

The mentor does not always look for a mutually beneficial relationship. He/she might just be paying it forward because he/she benefited from mentoring early on.

It is ideal that there is no direct working relationship between the mentor and mentee. Otherwise, the advice can be biased with the needs of the department or division where they work. The primary goal should be what is best for the mentee, not the company.

By the way, I personally avoid discussing the possibility of the mentee potentially joining my company or working directly under me. If that happens, he/she will have to look for another mentor.

The upside to having a CEO mentor is obvious. Many CEOs have "seen it all," and in their careers have experienced all sorts of setbacks, crises, and problems. If you find a CEO mentor from your own industry or a similar one, the lessons become more relevant. They can also help you make connections through their networks. Plus their war stories are most compelling.

There is a downside. Not all CEOs are trained to do mentoring or coaching. Fortunately, this is easy to learn through self-study or through established programs.

Finally, CEOs have limited time and want to make sure it is well spent. They are harder to find.

Why Mentor?

Mentoring, at first glance, is like a conversation between an uncle and their niece or nephew. The young person can talk to the uncle about issues they may not feel comfortable sharing with their parents. Uncles treasure the time spent with the young ones. It is one of the role's main joys. I know this from experience with my own relatives.

As a banker, I took on the task because it was the only way I knew how bankers were fully trained. At Citi, we were assigned mentors right from the start and it was natural for seniors to take juniors under their wing. It was just the way it was.

I have lost count of the number of managing directors and senior executives who started as junior officers in my care. I may not be in touch with them, but I know where they are, or I know where to find them. Their success is a source of pride.

Recently I discovered reverse mentoring! I did not realize this until I volunteered to mentor over 30 young people from various backgrounds on LinkedIn. There's also a select group of young professionals in the bank whom I brainstorm with, particularly about digital topics.

Now, I have thrown away some of my long-held beliefs. Now, I have to listen harder as the context is different. Generation gaps truly exist. Now, at 60 years old, I understand young people better — what their habits are, their dreams, what matters to them.

I have also learned to appreciate the emerging social needs resulting from the digital nature of their upbringing. Mentoring has given me much more satisfaction than I ever expected.

I am a better leader, I think, because of it.

Mentor Across Generations

After choosing 30 new mentees, I started to meet them in groups and one-on-one. At first, I began regretting why I decided to take on so many (I had over 200 applicants).

Thankfully, I learned from running a bank that people tend to have common needs and demographics which will simplify the process. I discovered that there are three "personas:"

First, the young professionals who are in the process of understanding themselves and starting to write their own story. I employ the triangle approach — what you enjoy doing, what you are good at, what the career opportunities are.

Second, the mid-careers who need to break through stagnation, reinvent themselves, or be more effective in their current roles. This is more complex.

The third are entrepreneurs/CEOs who think more about how to scale their businesses, although much about their start-ups is really about their personal brand. Sometimes they just need someone to bounce off ideas with. This takes much more time.

After each session, there is "homework" or what they need to think and do something about. They need to report in the subsequent session or by text.

Fortunately, I have been mentored or coached in the past across these three stages, and the process was robust. I attempt to implement the same frameworks whenever possible.

It has been personally gratifying meeting most of them, and in the process I learn more about myself. A neat extra benefit is that they get to meet each other and make new connections.

This makes it all worthwhile.

Inspire Junior Employees to Aspire

I was posed this question the other day by an HR officer: What to do with an employee who prefers to be part of the labor union and not be an officer? This had nothing to do with the dynamics between them and the union, it was purely a concern about a person's career.

First of all, it is the employee's right to have more faith in the collective bargaining agreement. If they feel safe that way, and if they do not aspire for supervisory positions for whatever reason, that is their decision. We respect that.

But what can HR do with what they see as "indifference?" My answer was that they had to prove their point. They have to sell.

There are enough career models to provide "proof of concept" to junior employees. Typically, many officers begin their careers as tellers/associates and they climb the ladder starting with being service officer and upwards. In fact, almost all my sales directors and regional service heads (VP to SVP) started from working behind the teller counters.

Stories of their career advancement are well-known in the branch network. During loyalty awards ceremonies, at least one of them is highlighted as a role model, and their speeches never fail to shed a tear.

These seniors, many of whom have spent decades with us, are more than veterans; they are living legends. Their careers inspire the young ones to dream of moving up to senior roles.

A favorite story of mine has to do with an employee who had to work her way through high school and college. During her early days as a teller, she gave her salary to her brother to pay off their debts. Last week, she was promoted to vice president.

Mentor Mid-Career Professionals

I must have mentioned in an earlier section that mid-careers have more complex issues, which makes conversations more interesting.

I initially refused to include them in my mentoring program, until I received half a dozen notes asking me to reconsider. The notes were long and persuasive.

The readers may be able to relate to three development issues:

1. I feel I am stuck — the person has been in the same role for so many years and has not seen progress. What makes it worse is that his peers have advanced. He feels that he has underperformed. This leads to inaction when there is no ownership or if the person blames others for his misfortune.

2. I feel alone — quite literally, he does not have lunch or coffee with anyone in the company. He has no friends. There is often a story behind this, a root cause that needs to be uncovered.

3. I am planning on leaving — usually this is the consequence of the first two plus the confluence of all other factors, especially the absence of advancement opportunities. When they call me, I always feel that they just need assurance that they are doing the right thing.

When I mentor, I want to help people take control of their situation and change it. After all, they already hold middle leadership positions and are even in charge of teams. I used to mock a course in my first bank that was called "self-leadership" or something like that. I was wrong. It turns out that the course is, in fact, very useful.

Let me be specific.

We feel stuck when we stop learning to improve our skills, or even simply to entertain ourselves. The same happens when we don't keep up with the trends. We are in a stage of massive transformation and disruption. We should see this as an opportunity for advancement. It is quite surprising that only a few take advantage of free training.

We feel alone when we don't make an effort to make friends. This has become more challenging with remote work. Join clubs, volunteer for collaboration projects. Dance or sing during Christmas parties and programs when new employees are being "initiated." If you find that this is beneath you, we need a serious conversation. I urge the lonely one to plant goodwill to harvest goodwill.

I may be old-fashioned, but I see nothing wrong with company events, generally speaking. I am surprised that there are plenty of articles that bedevil this practice.

Naturally, it helps if HR facilitates by providing self-service training opportunities and social activities, and imposes strict compliance to career advancement planning discussions. But the time for spoon-feeding is long over.

Take ownership of your career development. Don't wait for your manager to schedule a session with you.

A mid-career professional can go to the kitchen and feed himself/herself.

The good news is that these issues are in the minority. More of my time is spent discussing career options. Do I aspire for a general management role, or do I specialize? What are my alternatives? How do I evaluate an attractive offer from another company? These decisions are often new to mid-careers and are exactly what they need third-party opinion on.

And this is when I switch from coffee to white wine…

How to Reboot Your Career

Sometimes things do not go as planned. You see a dead end, or you feel stuck doing the same thing all over again. You are unhappy at work. Or you simply see a new opportunity you are missing. What do you do?

1. Do a root cause analysis of your situation. Why do you feel this way? Is it a problem with the industry? Your company? Your boss? The answer may not be obvious and you may need to ask "why" again and again, maybe five times until you get your answer. The conclusion might be that you need to seek another employment opportunity, but analyze first.

   Not all industries grow at the same rate. And within the same industry there are leaders and laggards. You cannot do much if you join a stale industry or company, except to leave and restart.

2. Find a best friend, or at least close friends at work. Do you have lunch alone all the time? That is a symptom. Friends make the work environment a bit more fun or less boring. Network with colleagues from other groups.

3. Learn something new. Get yourself certified in a skill that would help you move forward. Examine the industry trends and compare what is required against your current skills set. For example, being digital is the new minimum for bankers. Make yourself more valuable to your organization; at least your resume becomes more attractive.

4. Don't compare yourself with your best peers. There will always be someone doing better, for whatever reason, including getting the breaks. You might still be better than most of your cohort.

5. Find a mentor who can help you evaluate your options and navigate through ambiguity. Everyone goes through a rough patch; your mentor will be able to sympathize with you.

6. Get a life. Go to the gym. Find something new to do outside of work. Learn to play the saxophone or some instrument (I did, but I have since forgotten how).

I rebooted my career six times, excluding the time I decided to switch from physics to management through a scholarship from AIM.

The first was to specialize in derivatives to make myself unique in treasury. It was difficult to differentiate myself from other traders who were more senior both in the bank and in grad school, and who were already successful. I gained my managing director title through the derivatives path.

The second was to return to my home country at 45, become a local banker, and extend my shelf life while obtaining multiple new skills. I studied hard and bought six books before making this move.

The third was to move to a new employer that was more conducive to career development, and where my old Citi mentors were the main leaders. I found safety and the courage to do the fourth reboot.

The fourth was an adventure in mass market finance, initially by leading the acquisition of a consumer lending thrift bank, and later, four other companies focused on countryside banking and remittance.

The fifth was to go digital through 10 certification programs, to prepare me to rapidly lead the transformation of a new employer as their new CEO.

The sixth was to start writing regularly and redefine my role as an industry thought leader.

Whatever it is, start thinking and get moving.

Treasured Friends and Scalable Mentorship

One evening, bestselling author Eric Sim and I partnered for a fireside chat in front of two dozen CEOs and CHROs (chief human resources officers). Our topic was social leadership and our two books. The last time we had a gig together was probably in 2006, so I was looking forward to this LinkedIn-sponsored event.

Following Eric's introduction and questions, I explained that during the pandemic, LinkedIn's Philippine network reached a tipping point where active users now represented four valuable market segments: potential recruits, investors, corporate decision-makers, and affluent retail. In the past, my inbox used to be populated by the three Cs: club shares, condo, and computer/tech salespeople. Now, there is vibrant engagement on the platform.

My first takeaway is that we should always keep in touch with people who were with us during significant moments of our career. Surely the stories are rehashed a number of times, but they trigger parts of our brains that hold treasured memories. Eric read the first lines of The Beatles' song *Yesterday*, which I rewrote to explain FX options decades ago, but I was too shy to sing this time.

The second learning is that we keep building new connections, and these are often impeccably timed. I sat with the highly regarded CHRO of another bank and we had a long discussion on cutting-edge HR, but not before laughing about our shared experience that I expect we will always recount every time we meet.

Finally, I met Justin Koh, a young chap who follows my posts on LinkedIn. He remarked that I started scalable mentorship. I did not realize that I was doing exactly that. Now I will be more conscious about putting some structure into the material, the same way Eric organized his book into bite-sized insights.

I will do my best.

It Wasn't You

I recently just had lunch with a group of young leaders in the bank. One of them told me that a post I wrote many weeks ago hit her hard, as if it had been directed at her, bullseye.

The post was about long memos and the need to simplify. She remembered me writing in an email that I read her work during the entire ride home (about 40 minutes). She later (successfully!) cut it to one-and-a-half pages.

As a consequence, I have been indirectly mentoring this young lady, and she has been taking my comments constructively. Now, she considers it a form of torturous privilege that she laughs about. However, I can't recall intentionally plotting a LinkedIn post missile her way. Maybe it just came out instinctively as long, complex messages are a pet peeve of mine.

I am amused that, when some bank colleagues read my posts, they are convinced that the words were directed towards them, that it sounded deliberate. For example, my advice on promotion hit the spot. It made the rounds.

What's certainly happening is that my mentoring sessions are about problems that employees normally face. These are shared issues. When I write about them, readers can relate. The situation is familiar, they are able to put themselves in the shoes of the imaginary character.

This brings me to my earlier point on scalable mentoring. Any story that I write about can reach a much bigger crowd. One person's pain can become a lesson for many.

Maybe it was directed after all, although I prefer to call it collateral benefit rather than collateral damage.

Part Two

Outperform Your Peers

”

No one leads alone.

Chapter Five

Lead From the Frontlines

For a decade, when asked where my office was, I answered, "Where my BlackBerry is." After eight or so devices, I switched to an iPhone, but the habit remained the same. I visited hundreds of branches and clients during my tours of duty. Even at Citi, I preferred a trading desk and allowed people to use my office for meetings.

The pandemic forcibly changed my itinerary, but I went to 10 customer events around the country as soon as the situation improved. Leading from the frontlines was always my preferred approach.

CEO Undercover in Notting Hill

I wear a simple short-sleeve shirt or casual clothes when I go around the branch network to observe real, unscripted activities. This has given me invaluable feedback that I don't get from reports.

In my first CEO assignment, I saw how fast and polite our quickest teller was in a major branch. Then, I sat beside a customer who was distressed about an interbranch transfer from the province. We changed the slow process which previously relied on email advice. And I watched in shock when the computers in our Notting Hill office took forever to print a receipt. This was promptly fixed.

In my second local bank, I once caught the guards telling potential salary loan borrowers that they could no longer be serviced. I intervened before the customers could leave to go to another bank. Another time, the guard did not believe I was the chairman because I used an old car and looked too young for the position. People had a lot of laughs about that for years. I also tried to withdraw over the counter using my ATM card but the teller gave me all sorts of technology excuses.

Before assuming my current job, I opened an account in a small neighborhood branch while wearing a white collared shirt, red shorts, and topsiders. This did not work because someone suddenly called, "Mr. Acevedo!" It was a gentleman who recognized me from a recent social event.

These digital days, I frequently get messages on Facebook messenger, LinkedIn, and email when customers want to reach me. My undercover work has shifted online. I still try to do surprise visits, but as soon as one branch sees me, the whole area gets a message that "ESA is visiting branches."

It often becomes a game of cat and mouse.

Are You a Leader or a Manager?

I was truly sick of trainers who used this line in the '90s. I remember everyone lined up behind "leader" as if being a manager were a contagious disease.

Now, I think there is a consensus that you need to be both.

My view, which isn't original, is that leading is part of managing. Managers cannot be effective if they can't lead. Managers need to build skills in planning, organizing, leading, and controlling. POLC.

I learned this from Kepner-Tregoe manuals when, as a sixth-grade student in the '70s, I used to read my father's training materials when he was appointed a manager. Then I absorbed more from cases in graduate school.

Management has become more complex. Planning, for example, is now business strategy, with SWOT, the Porter model, and a gazillion frameworks. Organizing has subtopics like execution and human capital. Execution here means implementation, not death sentence.

Leading, by itself, has branched into executive coaching, 360-degree evaluations, and more, as leadership skills can be taught. Throughout my stay at Citi, I was subjected to a review by my supervisor, five of my peers, and five of my subordinates. Controlling has risk management and governance. Both have become rapidly expanding specializations.

But at the core, POLC still works for me.

Lastly, the higher up I moved, the more I was convinced that soft skills, like leadership, were what carried me upwards, and that leadership was about team leadership, not a one-man show.

Driving Charisma

The word can take on various interpretations, sometimes negative. I take it constructively to mean the ability to persuade people of the organization's vision. It is a crucial skill for leaders of teams that face unusual, uncertain, radical, and aggressive tasks.

I remember seeing a compelling article written by Harvard Business School's Nitin Nohria, Anthony J. Mayo, and Ranjay Gulati on this topic,where they referred to "inspirational visions" and "compelling personal attributes." (Ranjay Gulati was our professor on leadership during the Advanced Management Program. He gave us thick reading materials, all well-curated, and I have followed him ever since.)

There are times that call for this style of leadership, especially when the leader's enthusiasm needs to be contagious and must infect the middle layer, which forms the organization's influence spine.

However, apart from caring about people and the team at large, the vision being communicated needs to be credible. Emotional and nonverbal communication will not be sustained over time unless the message is logical and sound from a strategic or business standpoint. It has to make sense.

In a recent panel discussion, when I was asked what skill was required of CEOs facing a digital future, I replied "persuasion." I could have said charisma. Such is needed when you lead revolutionary change demanded by digital transformation.

When facing change, there will be a group of immediate adaptors. The opposite extreme will consist of non-believers. The mass of people in the middle is where you start preaching.

People need to believe.

Not a Rock Star

Charisma does not have to mean the rock star type. History has provided us with many examples of such personalities who practiced the economy of words, or may even be described as the total opposite of a charismatic individual.

I like how the traits were dissected in a LinkedIn collaborative article because they can be demonstrated by someone who is not an eloquent speaker. (I recommend reading these articles because, beyond the core points, industry experts also join in and contribute their views.)

Presence can be felt by simply being an active listener, understanding others' points, giving them time to speak.

Power can be quiet confidence, using the right words, backed up by competence.

Warmth can come out when authentic, by just being yourself.

Expressiveness follows when you are unscripted and give your honest views.

You need not put on a show. If you can, go ahead. But be yourself and ensure you know your stuff. Be truthful in those few instances when you don't have the solutions.

What is crucial, to me, is that the leader is persuasive because certain specific situations demand this skill. The absence of this ability will compromise his/her effectiveness. It is now a minimum requirement.

Charisma can take many styles. When used for the right reasons, it can move crowds and be powerful. When used badly, well, you know what happens.

Inspirational Leadership

One of the most influential speakers I have ever listened to was Emily Abrera. She used to head McCann and is a well-known personality in the business circles. (I sent her a note that I was going to write about this.)

I don't think she will really remember me, but her talk on inspirational leadership from a decade ago is still fresh in my head. Even if she delivered it without fanfare, it went very deep.

What I gathered from (or my version of) what she shared was:

Vulnerability — leaders have to be authentic. They can fail. They sometimes curse or are politically incorrect, but they show how they can recover from a fall. They are real people. On the other hand, invincibility and perfection are not relatable.

Insightful — slightly different from brilliance; this means leaders derive unique ideas from various situations as a result of their experience, learnings, and backgrounds. This also means listening to team members and distilling views into distinct strategies.

Courage — the determination to persist despite opposition and difficulty, against a number of odds.

Empathy — the tough type. Leaders need to demand performance and not coddle their teams, while caring for the team members. Tough love, in other words.

For easy recall, the acronym was VICE.

What I cannot remember is the number of times I used her lines. It must have been at least 50 times. I have yet to come across an article that explains inspirational leadership better.

Active Listening

When you grow up debating in school, or when you join an organization that behaves like a debating club, you are trained to be ready to respond to comments that you hear. The downside of this aggressive posture is that you spend less time understanding the message and the messenger's point of view.

As CEO, it is crucial to create a crew of collaborative experts that work together, that share insights, that watch for blind spots, that actively listen to build on each other's ideas.

Listening to understand, rather than to prepare for a rebuttal, is a glue that binds partnerships. It builds trust.

Under my Chairperson Helen Y. Dee, we have formed a solid group of leaders. Each one is an expert in his/her field. We broke down silos and made teamwork our main source of competitive advantage. Together, we have brought the bank to new heights, and transformed it across all the crucial parameters — financial, data science and analytics, digitization, sustainability, and financial inclusion.

It is a gift that keeps on giving.

This does not mean that we always have consensus. No. We frequently have conflicting views. What we agree on is how to find the answers, often through data. Even if one wins a few, and loses sometimes, overall the organization wins. Everyone wins.

This type of communication has permeated the lower levels of leadership. Officers from different groups and divisions enjoy the same professional camaraderie that their bosses have. This happened only because the senior leaders try to practice active listening across the bank. They model the desired behavior.

Delegation Builds Stars

To put it briefly, we encourage delegation to build future superstars and leaders.

Most professions, in addition to the required formal education, are a form of apprenticeship. To do well, you must learn from an expert, a master.

Delegation allows me to test my subordinates by giving them some accountability and sufficient authority to achieve a business objective. I will help them think about the task, but I will leave it to them, although I check in regularly.

This arrangement, over time, has evaluated technical competence, soft skills, and leadership potential of those under me. Better yet, I am able to identify their strong points and help them work on areas where they need to improve.

On the part of my younger colleagues, I hope that knowing their leader is watching out for them, acting as a safety net below, gives them the confidence to do their best.

By demonstrating delegation, I expect my one-downs to do the same with their teams. Over the years, I have consistently noticed that the best divisions are those that produce more superstars. I am concerned when I see leaders who do not have enough faith in their subordinates.

Management writers, in their analyses, refer to giving autonomy as a core ingredient in the process of creating leaders. They are probably right.

Who benefits? The leader actually benefits. When companies decide on upward mobility, it is easier to move leaders who have prepared worthy successors who can take over their jobs.

Public Speaking Engagements

Public speaking, like it or not, is part of a business leader's territory. However, given the limited time I have and my demanding day job, I have to choose which invitations to say yes or no to. It really depends on the topic and audience, and logistics.

I see a speech as a battle between the mobile phones in the crowd and me. There are minus points if the audience checks their messages. That is why the topic has to be entertaining while educational, and the delivery persuasive.

I will never speak on a subject that I have little background in. To me, it is dishonest if my speech is based on something I recently read and have no anecdotes and lessons to share. I am reminded of a company claiming to sell data science services many years ago. Their main presenter quoted from a page of a book I had read just days before. It was quite embarassing.

When the event is an opportunity to meet our target customer segments, the organizers are actually doing me a favor, especially if I have a ready set of slides. Even if it is designed for fellow bankers, I still accept it as I view it as my obligation to the industry.

A word on Zoom — it is virtually impossible to have audience engagement. The thing is, I like starting my talk by scanning the crowd, flashing a smile, and revising my opening line depending on the situation. With Zoom, it feels like I am talking to myself.

Finally, it is a matter of time management. The day job obviously takes priority, and out-of-towns are a challenge. But if it is a chance to meet new customers, it is hard to say no to. It is worth the trip.

Why I Write My Own Speeches

Over the last dozen years, I rediscovered writing. It started with being an editor in high school, but what really inspired me was a book on speeches that I found in college. That time, my favorite piece was Tony Blair's "I am proud, privileged, to stand before you..."

The problem was, believe it or not, I had to get over stage fright. Maybe this had to do with a badly done speech in sixth grade.

Over time, after much practice, I was set on the entertain, educate, persuade formula. And three main messages. I felt at ease, as making people laugh at some witty remark loosened me up as well.

I spend an hour or longer to write a two-page speech. For the really important engagements, I try to write a few weeks ahead, and then edit it twice more. I read it aloud to see if it sounds right. I watch out for tongue-twisters, polysyllabic words, and long sentences. I leave the introduction part blank or I put a default paragraph, preferring to personalize my first three sentences based on what I see and how I feel just before taking the rostrum.

It also helps build rapport when I mention certain personalities in the audience and share anecdotes about them.

It is hard to deliver what someone else wrote. The cadence is off. The rhythm changes. The words don't roll off my tongue smoothly.

Using my own material gives me more confidence. I find myself checking my text less, because I don't really need to memorize what came out of my heart and soul.

One last word of advice: When you start your speech, look into their eyes and begin with a wide smile. Be you.

It is Rhetorical

I have always been fascinated with how British pols speak eloquently. It turns out that they have a formula for it, and they practice it in their early years while in their exclusive schools. Then in Oxbridge. And then in the Parliament where there seems to be some order in the chaos. It indeed is an enviable skill.

I once watched a YouTube video on rhetoric and, while eating breakfast, wrote a piece in five minutes. Here it is, and imagine some stirring Churchillian drama while the words are spoken:

> CASA* consumer loans, cards.
>
> We will fight for new accounts.
> We will fight to cross-sell loans.
> We will fight to put cards in wallets.
>
> Yes we are small, but we have big fighting hearts.
> Yes we have had our share of troubles, but we now have momentum.
> And yes we have been wounded, but we are coming back strong.
>
> Our ship's sails have gathered wind, we are speeding through troubled seas.
>
> Bankers, this is the fight of our lives, we finally have the chance to be the country's best.
>
> Stand with me, be brave,
> It is victory we crave,
> Before us, you see,
> Is our goal, our des-ti-ny.

Always remember: three words or phrases, repetition, contrasts, metaphor, and exaggeration. End with rhyme. Thanks to Simon Lancaster's YouTube videos.

**Checking account and savings account*

Build a Meaningful Network

I grew up a shy boy, albeit with a ready smile. I was not antisocial, although I used to feel awkward at large events. Thankfully, I now often find a good number of friends and contacts whom I accept cocktail invitations from whenever I am free.

Who are in my network?

The first part consists of fellow bankers from the four groups I worked for, especially Citibank where I stayed for 23 years. Every time I meet them, we laugh about old stories and misadventures which we keep recounting *ad nauseam*. There are, literally, hundreds of them. In fact, half of the top 10 banks are led by Citibankers.

The second are customers I served early in my career when I was in treasury sales, and later when I became a senior banker. The junior officers I used to call on now occupy senior positions as well.

The third includes those I met in industry organizations or the academe, usually while volunteering for committees or working on common issues. Most of them are fellow bankers.

As an avowed introvert, I am comfortable with people I already know. It turns out that the ones I became close to were those I worked with on actual deals, projects, and other meaningful activities.

Collaborating with colleagues, taking on a sales role, and being active in industry organizations were what worked for me. These interactions "in the trenches" were the foundations of my friendships. This is one of the reasons why I strongly recommend taking a sales role.

As Shakespeare wrote in *Henry V*, "We few, we happy few, we band of brothers."

A Safe, Trusting, and Creative Environment

When holding meetings, it is important to convince attendees early on that they can feel safe, they will be listened to, and their opinions will be valued. It is already scary enough to meet the CEO for the first time. It is doubly frightening if the CEO looks serious.

I don't like diving straight into the agenda. Since people arrive 10 to 15 minutes early, we have time to catch up on personal updates, and get to know those I am meeting for the first time.

LinkedIn has also been useful in helping me check out their backgrounds. So yes, I do it.

In the bank, like in most companies, there is a succession plan for the critical positions. Meetings and projects are the best time to see future leaders in action. It is like a live interview. I think my teammates have already realized this. Every interaction with me is like a continuing interview. I make no apologies.

Interviews aside, meetings are primarily brainstorming sessions, even those meant for reports. When we build on each other's ideas, we arrive at insights that are far more compelling compared to those we might have concluded when working separately.

I have to admit that there are times when bad news has to be discussed. That is part of the job. In fact, it is an important part because, when the leader approaches setbacks constructively, it sets a positive tone across the company.

I want to leave the room feeling I learned something new and important, and that I got to know my colleagues better. I hope others leave feeling the same way, even if they are more relieved than happy.

If It Is Lonely At the Top, It Is Your Fault

They say it is lonely at the top because the buck stops with the CEO. The first part of the statement is true only if the second half holds.

I insist that leadership and loneliness don't belong together. At least, the new style of leadership has evolved from what I knew it to be decades ago, to a new version that is team-oriented.

Some of you might say, "Leadership is not a popularity contest; we need to get things done." But don't forget, leadership is about getting teams inspired to deliver results.

This is when I share what I have learned: that fear and harsh treatment of subordinates do not work. Fear stresses both the manager and the team, and all may perish from stress-induced cancer.

I am exaggerating, but what I really want to say is that you must engage the people under you, even those subordinates who do not like you and are your most severe critics (until they leave).

When decisions, or the process to arrive at decisions, are collegial, the burden is shared with other members of the leadership team. There is a higher chance of success when there is buy-in. The other benefit is that your colleagues better understand how you think and can anticipate your views. This is fine as long as they tell you what you need to know, not what they think you want to hear. There is significant difference between the two.

Obviously the primary accountability still rests with the man in charge. He carries this accountability, aware that his team is squarely behind him.

Offsite activities, instead of office meetings, create a more relaxed atmosphere. We hold this once a year for the management team, and another for directors.

Pressure to Perform

I was unwell for several days last week. With no good movies to watch, I clicked on two sports series: one on American football quarterbacks (QBs) and another on Formula One. There were lessons to learn from both.

In the first, there was incredible discipline on the part of the leader. The physical preparation on strength and agility was both scientific and high-tech. To be able to throw at the most unlikely angles required a flexible spine, for example. And since the defense always tried to sack the QB, he had to be put through rapid repair of injuries. As if this was not enough, he also had to study the plays diligently and cheer his team on. If the team had a bad record, or if the QB got injured, he was replaced.

It is Darwinian.

In races, the car had to be fast and robust enough to last the entire race, while the driver had to be very skilled. Both conditions had to exist for the team to score points. If the car underwhelmed, the manager was accountable. If the driver was unable to keep up with competition, he lost his seat. There was incredible burden for both to score.

Both sports were transparent. It did not take long to figure out where the problems were. The data was there for all to see. In both instances, the whole team had to get their act together to win. There is, undeniably, more pressure on the team leader and the manager. How does one perform under such weight of responsibility?

They started small, they started young. Then maybe they just got used to it. But the leader depended on the system around him to make him better, to help him recover, and to take his mind off the day job and relax.

No one leads alone. You win with a team.

Small Talk in the Frontlines

During my walk-arounds, I naturally get to talk to people. When I sit across from a teller, I try to lighten the mood by asking questions about her. How long has she been with us? Is she from the province? Where does she live? What about her parents? Where did she go to school? I am very particular about assigning people close to where they live, as shorter commutes improve work-life balance. During public transport strikes, or during very bad weather, there is a higher assurance that employees will be able to get to the office, and go home safely.

The last one I "interviewed" was, of course, a bit nervous when I sat near her. It turned out she joined from another bank which was acquired. I asked if she was happy and she gave me a smile while nodding, although I think she was happier when her supervisor walked over to "liberate" her from me.

There was a time when I used to ask about transaction counts and level of branch deposits, but I now limit those inquiries to branch seniors. Otherwise, I will have a reputation for giving oral exams.

In the bank, we have a robust training program for branch personnel. They attend the first formal program as service associates. The good ones move up to be trained again as service officers. If they want to switch to sales, they are nominated for the branch relationship officer bootcamp. From this group, we choose our relationship managers. If they stay in operations, they can be future service managers.

Even as we become digital, the branches will remain our center of gravity. They will evolve in terms of products served and skills required, but they will remain important in the foreseeable future.

Why I Walk Around the Bank

When I need to withdraw cash or run an errand, I sometimes do it myself to stretch my legs and gain about half a kilometer of walking. I take the elevator and go to the branch on the ground floor.

I find that it helps clear the mind, while giving me the chance to check the building and the branch — whether the ambience is warm and bright, whether the aircons are working, and if the plants still look fresh (or alive). I glance up at the ceiling (few people do), I look at the walls and furniture and the garden outside.

A particular concern of mine is waiting time. Second to traffic, branch queue is a major source of banking inconvenience. If customers wait more than 20 minutes, that means we are not following our standards.

I once thought of signature scents like what hotels have, but I have not made up my mind yet, probably because these come from a can while I prefer something natural. Anyway, I have realized that scent can be visual. A neat branch suggests to the brain that it smells good.

Sometimes I visit various floors. That stopped during the pandemic as we did not allow loitering.

What prompts this random act is usually an issue, or a problem that I haven't figured out, or where I think I am missing something. Have you thought of a problem before sleeping and woken up with a solution? That is why they say "sleep on it," but I cannot sleep on the job!

What I do instead is I "walk on it." Exposing my brain to visual sights probably unleashes the neural connections, the equivalent of kicking an old vending machine, clearing out the cobwebs.

Whatever the real reason is, I know that walking elevates my heartbeat and pumps more blood to my brain. It works for me.

"I Didn't Expect a Reply"

I am often told that line when I reply to messages on LinkedIn, Facebook Messenger, and email. I have always thought that replying is the polite thing to do when someone makes an effort to reach out to me. There is nothing special about my gesture.

Some of these are customer complaints and suggestions which are quite helpful. I am able to address them promptly. I am grateful for new ideas, and I apologize for any inconvenience.

Others ask for mentoring, although I regret that the line-up is already full. I still answer their questions, unless they ask me for longer insights which I can't accommodate. I just advise them to refer to my previous posts instead. I have to say though that when I find an extraordinary young person, I will make room in my schedule. This is how I ended up with 30 instead of 10 mentees as originally intended.

I also answer those looking for work, although googling "RCBC Careers" is faster. I sometimes look up interesting resumes. I endorse to HR only those I personally know and can vouch for.

Some offer me work, I kid you not. Then a handful asks for a fistful of money.

Like most of you, I don't respond to real estate and club share agents, or any similar salespersons. I know they send hundreds of messages anyway and expect only a tiny percentage to respond. I am helping to keep the statistics to a low single digit.

Despite the courtesy that I extend, there are rare instances when I come across problematic individuals. When that happens, the only solution is to block them.

Join Audit and See the World; How to be Ahead of Auditors

I was a traveling treasury auditor during the year my employer transitioned to the risk-oriented audit approach. This was helpful as I got to understand businesses more broadly and deeply. The downside was that I later often got assigned to fix units that failed audit reviews. It was a small price to pay for the opportunity to work in Seoul, Taipei, Tokyo, Hong Kong, Kuala Lumpur, London, and Sydney for two to four weeks at a time.

The auditors' three main tasks are (1) to identify the main risks in your business or department, (2) to ensure those risks are mitigated or subjected to appropriate controls, and (3) to test the controls. As someone on the business side, you will need to know the same set of three tasks. In fact, you should know them better, deeper than auditors do. Running a business, after all, includes controlling.

Risk identification needs to be a yearly exercise. This can be more frequent when you introduce new dimensions — new products, new customers, new technology, new procedures. New = uncertainty = risk. New risks need to be calibrated to ensure they are worth taking.

The decision to take new risks depends on your ability to mitigate them, or set up effective controls. And you will need to ensure that the persons in charge of the new control procedures understand the risks and are diligent in their roles.

When an auditor files a comment, always check against the rule book. You will learn something new. If the comment deals with minor, insignificant matters, argue that the controls are still generally effective.

Finally, be courteous. Auditors respect officers who know their business well. At the end of the day, it is about documented confidence.

”

When you want to please everybody, you end up pleasing nobody.

Chapter Six

Forge a Compelling Strategy

I learned strategy early in my career, but I credit Harvard Business School Professor Cynthia Montgomery for teaching me, decades later, how leaders can shape corporate strategy based on the company's core values and purpose, and design a consistent and compelling plan of action around that core.

The best part about starting with values is that you begin with why the company exists; the strategy flows logically from that.

The Leader as a Strategist

Last year, I was asked by an organization of Catholic schools to speak on strategy. Since education is my favorite personal cause, I immediately agreed.

A bit of background first. In my country, Catholic schools are known for providing quality education. However, over the past 10 years, the government has made it a priority to increase salaries of public school teachers. The latter are now generally paid more than their private counterparts. As a result, private schools are losing veteran teachers.

When preparing the material, I asked myself these questions: What value does the school give to the community? What will the enrolled families miss if the school closes? The answer was obvious: provide high-quality education. This, of course, was something close to the hearts of parents.

To deliver this value, the school has to recruit and retain well-trained teachers, prepare a transformative curriculum, spruce up facilities, among others. All these cost money. The school needs to prepare a financial plan that will enable them to pay higher teacher salaries.

This plan might include reducing the number of non-teaching personnel, outsourcing some non-core services, using external facilities for non-core activities, and seeking government subsidies and post-grad scholarships. I wrote all these on a single PowerPoint slide.

I followed what I learned exactly 10 years ago. Professor Montgomery proposed that strategy starts with declaring the company's value or purpose at the core, and is then surrounded by various components (like finance, human resources, marketing, operations, etc.) that support the core. The attendees appreciated the plan because it hit the spot and did not sugarcoat the problems. They murmured their approval. I am sure they already thought about some of the things I wrote; they were just unable to make the case confidently.

Five years ago, when we had a longer list of things to fix in the bank, I wrote the 10 tasks which the press started calling the Ten Commandments. I was even referred to as "Moses" at some point. The objective was #fightto5, or climbing back to fifth place among private universal banks. The list was not the easiest to remember, although the hashtag was catchy, but we had other reasons for doing it that way.

As soon as we completed half the tasks, and through animated brainstorming sessions, we were finally able to agree on our goal and our plans.

Our challenger bank strategy now consists of an objective and four components referred to as the ABCDs — Acquire new customers, Best customer experience, Current and savings accounts, and Digital transformation. Each letter has three corollary action plans. Over time, these plans have evolved, but the ABCDs have been steady for four years now.

A strategy is useless unless widely communicated and understood by people assigned to implement it. Therefore, it needs to be clear and concise, and easily shared. Even those of large, complex companies can be summarized so that everyone understands the direction the company is taking. On a single PowerPoint slide.

To me, the next most critical task is ensuring that middle managers can transmit the overall strategy. And they should be able to craft their divisions' own specific plans to support the company's goals.

Finally, whenever he can, the CEO has to go on the road to talk and listen to the troops. When targets are ambitious, when there is a feeling of doubt, the CEO's presence becomes imperative to boost confidence in the plans.

The message is best delivered in person.

Just Do It

I was chatting with someone who told me how she was so impressed with entrepreneurs from an Asian territory decades ago. They just jumped into business opportunities without much analysis and quickly reaped the benefits.

I read a similar account about a pioneering tech company which never had the time to prepare a business plan even after being in operation for a number of years. They just kept on working hard to stay ahead.

Both situations had massive demand opportunities that had to be met immediately. Both sets of entrepreneurs had the skills and resources to meet the demand. Maybe that gave them confidence to take the leap forward. They were "agile" before it became a buzzword.

The other point is that we generally never hear stories about the ones who failed. As they say — dead men tell no tales.

I am tempted to analyze the stories of the successful ones as a combination of many factors, or even calculated risk. Instead, to honor these brave souls, I will refrain from studying them.

I have kept repeating a mantra that Professor Fred Pascual drilled into my head decades ago: that a high-risk business strategy must be accompanied by a conservative financial plan. Otherwise, there is little room for error, especially if an error has substantial consequences.

When assessing a borrowing customer, that always comes to mind. And when I meet young financial officers, I try to bring this into the conversation.

When Plan A is bold, liquidity allows you to regroup during setbacks and launch Plan B.

Science and Leadership

Several weeks ago, I wrote about how, in the bank, we have been using the word "hypothesis." We go through data to verify our thoughts. We experiment.

This should not be surprising because the leadership team has a strong science background, with about half having majors in physics, chemistry, biology, psychology, statistics, or engineering. We are ready to accept that we can be wrong. In fact, I get excited when data and experiments overturn initial beliefs. By being open, we have found insights that were contrary to traditional banking wisdom and practices.

We need to encourage a culture of experimentation, especially when the consequence of failure is low and manageable. We must avoid over-controlling, with too many rules that are often hard to remember. Instead, we set boundaries or parameters that are easy to follow, and allow freedom for managers to exercise creativity within those boundaries.

Recently, I attended a webinar organized by one of the leading global consulting firms. I smiled when the speaker, a best-selling author and professor, spoke about almost exactly the same concepts, using the same words.

Indeed, as we transform, as we go where leaders have never gone before, we need to unlearn and be ready to accept new wisdom.

Nowadays, in the digital environment, we make bets — intelligent ones — and we have to move fast. We no longer have the luxury of time to write long analyses. The decision process has to adjust to the new realities.

We are not even sure what the future ideal will look like.

Looking for Clarity

The other day, one of my younger group heads asked for an urgent meeting to discuss a situation which had two conflicting alternatives. The project team was inclined to follow what appeared to be safe and proper, with a superior financial result.

I disagreed and overruled. My reason was simple. The chosen alternative, while attractive, was not consistent with our bank's values. The second plan of action, on the other hand, fit our values perfectly, even if it was going to cause some inconvenience.

My colleague smiled and understood immediately.

Life does not consist of business cases to solve. Life does not give you problems compartmentalized according to topics. You do not get them in your IN box. Life is complex.

To look for clarity, you first need to understand the environment as deeply as you can, and assess how your company can respond. Managers use SWOT and other methods that do exactly that, as they help organize the available information.

What next? This is where the company's core values or their "purpose for existence" becomes the point of reference. How the company deals or interacts with its environment should be consistent with its values.

This is exactly what happened in my interaction with my subordinate. Nowadays, some people refer to their "True North." I am happy that it works for them.

In our case, it is simply staying true to what we stand for. When in doubt, I refer to the values of our founder, Ambassador Alfonso Yuchengco.

Preserve Corporate DNA

In smaller companies, the company's DNA is the owner's DNA. As the company grows, and when there is close proximity of offices, how the owner and the first employees behave and conduct their business becomes the norm, without the need for formal training or manuals.

However, during periods of rapid expansion, there is a risk of culture dilution as new employees are hired, or as distance makes regular contact difficult.

Let's take a practical example. For financing companies, culture will include a set of principles and the way they behave when dealing with borrowers and going about credit practices and collection routines. I have been involved with a number of these companies and have several clients I regularly discuss with. I have observed that the following methods are common:

1. There is formal training for new staff. And both formal and informal ways of networking across the organization.

2. Branch expansion teams consist of veterans who train new offices on-the-job. They promote seasoned leaders to lead new outlets and model culture. These leaders have a strong connection to the head office.

3. They audit new offices early to check whether company practices are consistently applied.

4. They share customer service stories and celebrate exemplary behavior. Leaders make time to conduct town halls.

The approaches are similar and the effort is sustained, as leaders understand how important culture is.

Learn From the Best (Opponents)

Banking is an extremely competitive industry, even before adding fintechs to the mix. Naturally, we adhere to Sun Tzu's advice: learn as much as we can about our opponents.

In particular, we study whoever is the best in each business category. The best in credit cards is not the same as the best in auto loans or home loans. We base our assessment not just on top-line numbers but also on product subcategories.

We find out about their strategy. What is their marketing mix? Digital marketing tactics? Digital channels? Sales incentives to dealers? Direct sales? How did they transform their business? Do they have "11 herbs and spices?"

I admire many of our competitors. We have been chasing them over the last five years and we learned more by racing from behind; it is a great vantage point. Like following the peloton leader in the Tour de France, racing from behind reduces friction while we prepare to surge forward with our own plans.

How can we improve ourselves to get closer to them? How can we build a similar capability? And finally, what can we do differently that will give us an edge?

Industry events give us an opportunity to compare notes, particularly in digital initiatives undertaken. This is where most of the effort is concentrated nowadays.

Naturally, we also study our customers, substitute products, and new entrants. We "scout," as sports fans would say.

Welcome to the game.

Boldly Going

I am naturally risk-averse as a person and as a banker. I have been told that many times. But I have also been a trader, structurer, and treasurer for two decades, leading trading rooms in Manila and Hong Kong. Does that make sense?

It does, because the type of risks we were taking were quantifiable based on normal market volatility and stress events, which were becoming usual. The risks were generally known.

Lending is entirely different, as I have learned over the last 15 years. Each company and its managers are unique, even if it helps to compare those in the same industry. Each individual is distinct, although it is possible to classify people into several buckets (of similar score or risk).

But one thing is certain: when we identify safe sectors or those where the risk-return is attractive, we push aggressively. Looking for the sweet spot is key. When we find it, we boldly go where few have gone before.

However, I struggle with the concept of lending to digital start-ups because they have no positive cash flow. If the business strategy falls short of expectations, cash quickly runs out. These companies are usually funded by owners, friends, and family, and subsequent equity rounds. No bank is, generally, willing to lend until there is actual cash flow. This can take five to seven years, I am told.

What about using the value of intellectual property as collateral? I was asked this question at least twice. Sure, but intellectual property with no cash flows cannot service a loan.

There is a chance that the start-up will do well, even if the failure rate is 75% (even higher for blockchain companies). The ones that thrive can enjoy spectacular gains. To be specific, the shareholders get those profits, not the lenders, unless the loan carries equity-type gains.

There are investors who specialize in these types of endeavors. They are aware of the risks, and they take these risks with eyes wide open.

Don't Miss a Marketing Opportunity

One Valentine's Day, the coffee shop next door decided to be creative and baked strawberry-flavored, heart-shaped donuts. They looked really yummy. Great idea, I thought. I smiled.

Then I saw that they sold the treats at 2 for 90 pesos. An average price of 45 pesos each. Quite unimaginative. I was disappointed.

Why only two when the universally-accepted number for love is three pieces? I had to take action. I went to the manager and suggested: 3 for 143. An average price of 47.67 pesos, and they sell faster with more margin.

I did not need to explain the obvious. The number 143 is the numerical shortcut when you want to express your affection, at least in my generation. The young ones know what it means, even if they find it corny.

I left the coffee shop without knowing whether they followed my recommendation. They probably ran out of goodies before they could make the price change. Or someone bought a dozen which, I admit, is a more powerful number.

I have been trying to avoid flowers as they wither within days. There was a year when I gave 100 small teddy bears. I can still find them displayed in cubicles. They sold for three dollars each. That costs less than a single Ecuadorian rose.

While I make light of pricing strategy, it is actually a science in itself. You will know when you buy a ticket just a few days before your flight. Or when you book a room with only a week to go. The price dynamically adjusts. It is partly economics; there is generally less supply, and you appear desperate.

This is just one component of the marketing mix. There are more to consider.

Ensure Successful Business Transformations: The Five Components

Most books talk about digital transformation as it is the sexy part. They dive immediately into digitizing the core business and the subsidiary strategies. I believe what they say, since they actually hold true. However, from my experience, digitization cannot exist in isolation. A total of five transformations have to happen.

Briefly:

First, we reassess the business model to sharpen the strategy. What value are we providing and for whom? Go after high-growth customer segments with a scalable strategy, and a solution that is better than what the market currently provides. Staff appropriately.

Second, use industrial engineering tools to cut turnaround times, lessen documentation, and reduce transaction cost. Be more efficient.

Third, employ digital tools. Use a digital onboarding channel. Digitize the middle and back offices. Aim for straight-through processing.

Fourth, further elevate customer experience using data science, personalize targeting niches, and use credit scores and other models to make decisions instantaneous.

Fifth, ensure that the workforce adopts a new agile, customer-obsessed culture from problem identification to ideation, and with collaboration across groups.

The first two are traditional methods. The next two are possible because of faster and cheaper computing capacity. But in the end, people make transformations happen, and sustain them. People and culture make the difference.

For business transformation to thrive, we need all five.

Sail into the Wind

I first thought that sailing against the wind was nonsensical. When I saw it on TV, I started being fascinated with the concept because common sense suggests that it is virtually impossible. And it is rich with analogy, i.e., moving forward despite resistance and difficulties.

For starters, you really cannot sail directly against the wind. You move sideways into the wind.

Through science and skill, sailors can make the boat move forward into a headwind by going diagonally and creating a net forward movement by using physics.

The sail acts like a wing that gives the airplane a lift. In the case of the sailboat, the same action tends to move it sideways. The boat's keel (the perpendicular board below) converts the sideways movement into a forward motion. This is hard to describe even with a drawing. The best way to study this is by checking YouTube videos.

I was in a sailboat one afternoon and watched the skipper in action. He instructed me to compare the direction of the wind as indicated by a flag versus the path we were taking. He described the maneuver in simple words while I sipped on my Carib.

I tried to contain my enthusiasm as I listened to the lesson. It actually worked!

I shared this story with one of my senior leaders whom I knew was raised in a town beside Taal Lake. He smiled and shared that his father, a fisherman, did exactly that maneuver.

Whenever business conditions become tougher than usual, I get reminded of that trip in the islands.

The E=MC² of Business

I grew up studying the sciences and later the business of banking. I was always on the lookout for ways of simplifying my understanding of business models. I thought I finally found it when someone showed me this:

Profit = Volume x (Price – Cost)

In other words, to increase profit, you need to generate more volume, raise prices, and manage down cost.

In reality, under intense competition and with new entrants, prices tend to come down over time. Unless you have a premium product or a new offering that is unchallenged, you assume there is little room to maneuver. Gravity wins.

Cost, on the other hand, has more flexibility.

With digitization, you can migrate from face-to-face to cheaper digital channels. With AI, you can multiply employee productivity, thereby expanding capacity without raising headcount. And with strategic choices, you can cut the cost of credit and collection, and cost of customer acquisition.

To me, the most crucial component is volume growth. That is where you can deliver the most value.

Go after higher-growth markets. Offer a superior product that encourages customers to switch from their current suppliers. Invent new services that solve customer pain points. Be obsessed with improving the customer experience. Targeted marketing through analytics. Wholesale acquisition of customers. Cross-sell more products to your existing customers. Performance management of the salesforce. And discover advocacies that inspire your troops.

There are many ways.

Pressure, Diamonds, and the Price of Love

Pressure is one of the concepts I often apply in business when explaining strategy focus and market segmentation. In physics, it is the perpendicular force applied on an object per unit area. Pounds per square inch, for example.

When you apply focus on a wide area, you achieve less. Effort, when distributed over a big surface, is diminished. But the same quantity of force dedicated solely on a small point can puncture. Like kung fu artists who can damage livers using a bent pointed finger to the chest of the unfortunate stunt man, provided the right breathing techniques precede the punch.

A business must choose market segments it wants to penetrate and not try to be everything for everyone. Different customer personas possess different sets of needs. Truly, when you want to please everybody, you end up pleasing nobody.

Finally, I have been reading about laboratory diamonds. And on my visit to Central Luzon months ago, a lady told me that her family's business sells jewelry that uses lab diamonds from India, and the prices are much cheaper than natural diamonds. They actually declare that their diamonds are "lab-grown." Was I pleasantly surprised. And she confirmed that natural and lab ones cannot be distinguished. After all, diamonds are carbon plus pressure. The latter can be simulated in a manufacturing facility.

I was intrigued and tried to find out how the industry responded. When the diamond cartel had to explain the huge price difference between the two types of engagement rings, the spokesperson argued: "How can you put a price on love?"

That's when I knew that one side was in trouble.

Growing Organically or through Acquisition

Organic growth means increasing business size using existing resources. A company, by default, already tries to grow organically, and can always choose to scale up the effort.

A bank, for example, will hire more staff, open more channels to reach customers, attract more customers with higher deposit rates, and give incentives to employees to ramp up sales. There are minimal change, cultural, and systems issues, provided all three are well-managed.

Accelerating organic growth costs money and requires training of new hires, but is much cheaper than buying companies, unless one gets reckless with aggressive lending and loose credit standards.

The downside is that organic growth generally takes much longer, and the company has to do its own R&D.

On the other hand, acquisitions boost business size and market share immediately. It brings in new products that can be sold to existing customers and markets. New expertise will benefit the combined company. There will also be opportunities for synergy, including the ability to cut overhead.

The difficult part has to do with cultural differences, which require deliberate employee assimilation and retention programs. There is significant danger of employee and customer attrition. Defending against these costs money. As companies become more digital, the integration of systems becomes more complex. Doing this exercise is worth the effort. Delaying it just leaves land mines for the future.

When buying companies, the cash outlay can be quite significant. There are exceptions. During "shotgun mergers" sponsored by western regulators to rescue ailing banks, the surviving entity often had to shell out minimal money, but had to deal with a multitude of legal problems afterwards. There may be "skeletons in the closet," like inherited legal issues in US mergers during the GFC (global financial crisis).

An acquisition has to bring something new that the company either does not have or will take long to build internally. Otherwise, the acquirer is simply buying time.

Which path to choose depends on the company's strategic intent and capacity to manage growth. In the Asian setting, banks have relied on acquisitions to move up in the leaderboard. I doubt this will change.

Instead of banks buying other banks, I now see them acquiring fintech start-ups and consumer finance companies. The main idea is that the acquirer can immediately monetize the new products, or they are convinced that they can run the new businesses more efficiently.

Four years ago, we merged our thrift bank with our universal bank. It took over a year of preparation. I learned from that experience, and from eight other deals I have been part of in the past. The most difficult part had to do with people. Technology came next.

Acquisitions don't always look good in the early stages as reality sets in and euphoria comes down. This is because it is difficult to manage varying emotions, and unease creeps in. My investment banker friends call it "buyer's remorse."

In the end, employees and leaders have to stay the course. Don't stop believing.

Game, Theory, and Game Theory

Whenever we discuss adjustments to our business strategy or tactics, we need to think about other banks, how they act now, and what they are capable of doing next.

There is fun in competition. There are industry leaderboards and awards, although there is nothing better than a great rating in a customer survey (assuming financials are okay).

We can never be completely sure of why and how customers and competition are acting exactly at present. And what their motivations are. Looks can be deceiving. There cannot be a single story for customers; it is better to think of them as belonging to several groups (personas) where members behave similarly.

Competing companies, on the other hand, have reasons why they act a certain way. And we have theories or hypotheses which can be confirmed later in the future. We know them, after having studied them long enough.

We must anticipate how other parties will react when we make certain moves. It is naïve to assume that they will stay the same. They will likely respond to our shift in strategy. This will affect our expected outcomes.

It gets complicated. A series of actions and reactions can sometimes be destructive for an industry, like a war of attrition. Conversely, it can also be win-win. A good example is how banks have gotten together and built automated clearing houses which allow for interoperable payments. There is cooperation in the middle, but there is competition around it.

In 2010, a foreign bank played cute and offered home loans at 5.99%. Since their loan book was tiny, it was of little consequence even if it was noisy. The big banks did not follow as it was costly to do so. We responded with 5.55%.

Suppliers as Partners

When I say "partner," I am referring to suppliers that have made an effort to deeply understand what we do, have served us for years/decades, and have built personal relationships with my colleagues. Our business is obviously important to them, but I also believe that being with them makes us more competitive.

This does not mean that we welcome everyone. In fact, this means we need to be discriminating. We choose. We focus on what our customer pain points and strategic priorities are, and look for partners we can collaborate with.

At least two new tech suppliers believe weekly, that they have a solution to my problems. I usually politely ask them to send the note to my CTO instead. Or, if they have an interesting proposition, send me a file to read.

This week, I saw the best and the not so good. Yesterday, I had lunch with an audit firm leader who likes to catch up on our strategy, asks questions, and tells me how he thinks his firm can help. No hard sell.

Earlier this week, I gave another company a piece of my mind because I was disappointed with their support. My honesty was received well. Partnerships enable you to quickly fix setbacks, as communication lines are well established.

But the best part I like about partnerships is the collaboration that results from it. Case in point: our Singapore-based friend who always comes up with one great idea after another. Home run after home run.

When you treat your partners well, they help you with great insights. They call you first when they have a big idea. They want you to succeed.

It is really no different from being on the same team. We all win together.

Who Reads Annual Reports

As a grade-school kid, I looked forward to the annual reports of the company my father worked for. I always went straight to the page that showed the directors and senior officers, as if the report were a book with colored pictures. To my young mind, each person had a story — where he went to school, if he graduated with honors or did his MBA abroad, what his other positions were, what other boards he sat in, plus other interesting info. Back then, the company owners hired executives who went to Wharton, where most family members studied.

It was as if I knew each one of them intimately. If there were an exam about them, I could have gotten a perfect score.

The letters of the president and the chairman were the second most interesting parts as they summarized national and corporate developments. Since I had no financial background then, the balance sheets and income statements were not relevant to me (now I check them first before anything else).

The production quality of these reports has vastly improved through the years as stories are now told better, messages are organized around a central theme, and even pictures are taken in a way that is consistent with the overall look.

Who reads them? According to the Vienna University of Economics and Business, the company's employees made up one-fourth of all the readers, which means, based on rough calculations, most of them don't bother. Analysts (17%) and private shareholders (12%) are the expected audience. And then 14.5% by students and job applicants. Customers make up 8%. Only 7% are journalists, sustainability experts, and NGOs.

The only problem with these reports now is that the pictures are taken after my birthday celebrations, but I am digressing.

How to Convince Customers to Switch

Somehow, every customer worth pursuing is already spoken for. Someone is already serving their needs. To win their business, you have to convince them to switch. How?

The quick answer is by providing a product or service that solves a problem better than what your competition offers. And it has to be materially better, enough to convince the customer that the hassle of switching is worth suffering through.

It is easier when your product becomes added to the customer's list as an alternative or substitute. Then you can gradually eat market share away from incumbents. Loans, cards, and deposits are examples. In the bank, we do this through new offerings like payroll advance or credit card installment conversion, both through the app.

In our payroll advance service, the customer can take a loan in less than two minutes. Credit card installment conversion is done in a few clicks. Our competitors are still working on an equivalent product offering. We have to keep improving ours as well.

But there are services that are entrenched. Like payroll or collection. Conversion to a new supplier is messy and takes so much effort. What tilts the balance is bad customer service from existing providers. If the customer is already suffering, or someone makes him realize he has been miserable, the decision to switch is easier to make.

Customers can only take so much bad service. It is crucial that we keep reviewing our own products and keep improving, because standards keep rising. We need to be better than competition, but we should also be better, as marketing guru Josiah Go once stated, than what we were yesterday.

Homework Before Meeting a Client

Apart from knowing about the client's business and services that we provide, I look up the main decision-makers on Google, LinkedIn, and other social media. There might be connections I have that I am not aware of.

For example, if we went to the same school, have the same major, have similar interests and hobbies. In some countries, being raised in the same part of the country and speaking the same dialect is a powerful door opener. Hence, I speak the dialect whenever I can.

I once faced a local tycoon in Mindanao who, I wasn't aware, was planning to repay our loan and rebook it with another bank. When I found out, I reminded him that I was raised not very far from where we were, and that the bank was not going to let him down. He stayed with us.

The first objective in a client meeting is to build a relationship. Business comes second. In some meetings, depending on the client, business is discussed only during dessert and coffee, an afterthought.

This is why I prefer that proposals be sent or worked on before the meeting, and then use the meeting to move the proposal forward.

I will need to have a short pitch to follow through, stating that we believe we can offer the service better than their current providers can. If it is an existing relationship, I ask what else we can do, anything that we can work on for them.

Finally, it is also good to fix the logistics. If we are meeting in a restaurant, and if I have time, I check the restaurant's menu ahead. If I am unfamiliar with the location, I use Waze to estimate travel time.

Client time must be quality time.

”

If the deal scares you, it is probably worth doing.

Chapter Seven

Turn Losses into Wins

Almost every competitor in sport starts by being at or near the tail end. No one starts at the top. In fact, Roger Federer was once asked if he still remembered the boy who gave him a 6-0, 6-0 thrashing. What differentiates winners is that, despite the losses, they practice, they learn, they evolve, they get better.

It is the same with your career. You can't move forward unless you stick your neck out to compete. You can't build your skills without investing time in learning. No pain, no gain.

What to Do When I Have a Bad Day

When I have a bad day, my secretary asks if I want garlic parmesan chicken wings from my favorite fast food restaurant. The answer is often a "yes." It comes with pasta sometimes, or pizza depending on whether I am on a keto diet. Sometimes, I ask for a bowl of ramen.

But what I almost always do is tidy up my office and move things around.

I scan old pending papers in the IN box, go through my email and physical folders, cull old material, and move the decor around. Shredding was therapeutic until my secretary insisted on doing it herself. There is something about the shredding sound that soothes.

My response to emails and memos follow the Eisenhower Matrix where the urgent tasks like transaction approvals are done within minutes unless in a meeting, those I need to read and think about for later goes to the pending file, tasks I pass on to lieutenants, and those I delete. A bad day is when I go back to types 3 and 4. Some messages turn out to be entertaining, so it helps.

While I do this, I sip coffee. I do not touch alcohol.

If this does not improve my mood, I walk around the building. During really terrible times, I escape and have a massage. Or even go to my barber. I am back within an hour and a half.

Doing "low-brain" activity destresses me. It also makes me recall pending items long forgotten, which provides a necessary distraction.

Finally, an uncluttered desk with a cup of sharp pencils is a reminder that I can restart with a clean slate.

If It Scares You

Yesterday, one of my colleagues asked for a meeting to discuss something face-to-face. I was curious and agreed.

He described what he planned to do, but I could see a different expression, something I never saw before. I asked if it was making him anxious. He nodded.

The biggest, most important deals I worked on frightened me, I told him. My first acquisition worried me endlessly, even if it turned out to provide a payback quicker than everyone expected. My most profitable derivatives deal made me very nervous that I forced myself to calm down so I could think better. Presentations to large audiences also made me anxious for days. Over time, I got more relaxed and became used to the process.

Our nervous system is wired to warn and prepare our ancestors against risks lurking in the African savannah, where a leisurely walk can be your last. Thousands of years later, it still fires up the same way when triggered by modern peril. Or maybe our ancestors' brains reacted that way when hunting for big game.

Sit down and think clearly, I counseled, go through it a number of times. Sleep on it. Ask for advice. Then I encouraged him to go for it. I would do the same if I were in his place, I said.

After my sharing and mini lecture, I ended by saying something that I repeated many times over the last two decades: "If the deal scares you, it is probably worth doing."

Happy hunting!

Defeat and Courage

As a history nerd, I used to wonder why most cultures celebrated epic defeats. Like Remember the Alamo, Thermopylae, the Fall of Bataan. And the Gallipoli Peninsula. Even Hollywood has embraced them.

Of all the tragic routs, one stands out in memory.

In elementary school, I first heard of Alfred, Lord Tennyson's *The Charge of the Light Brigade*, where 600 rode into the valley of death. The actual scene was the Battle of Balaclava in the Crimean War. The Light Brigade, because of a misunderstanding between commanders, charged against Russian artillery that was well-positioned. They were forced to retreat after taking heavy losses.

As I grew older, I realized it was not about defeat, it was about remembering courage. Falling while fighting against all odds is a triumph of the human spirit.

As Lord Tennyson magnificently wrote:

> "Theirs not to make reply,
> Theirs not to reason why,
> Theirs but to do and die.
> Into the valley of Death
> Rode the six hundred."

On a separate note, during a visit to Victoria, I spent hours at the ANZAC Museum — the Shrine of Remembrance. Young men who were farmers, teachers, and ordinary folk volunteered to enlist and never returned. They paid the ultimate sacrifice.

Finally, in case you wanted to ask, the balaclava headgear worn in cold weather originated from the Battle of Balaclava. British troops wore knitted headgear to keep warm.

Resilient Leaders

Most young professionals never lived through a crisis until COVID struck. Thanks to a near-balanced budget, my country was relatively immune to the GFC from 2008 to 2009, and SARS never made a dent in 2002.

On the other hand, those now in their 50s and 60s went to school during the country's first debt restructuring, started working when coups were frequent, and in their 30s suffered through the Asian crisis.

If you worked for a US company, there was this added real estate crisis in the mid-90s. And if you were an expat in Hong Kong and Singapore, there was SARS in the early 2000s.

I remember how it felt, and what my company's leaders did to survive and thrive. I recall taking a whole-day trip to an export processing zone to restructure a deal. We spent hours convincing a footwear exporter to honor their foreign exchange trades. I can't forget squaring off positions and fixing our funding one evening in the trading room before the coup rebels overtook the business district. Good thing our pantry was well-stocked with crackers and cheese.

I still think about how I once called my entire Hong Kong treasury team to a Sunday meeting in November 2008, fearing we may all be jobless the following week. (The Fed came to the rescue.)

This morning, I read that there is further escalation in the Middle East, raising the risk of inflation.

It helps that organizations are now led by men and women who went through hell several times before. They have been tested.

Two Kinds of Pain

In the very first scene, my second favorite character from *House of Cards*, Francis Underwood, famously declared, "There are two kinds of pain. The sort of pain that makes you strong, or useless pain. That sort of pain that's only suffering."

That first episode (and yes, Robin Wright) convinced me to watch the rest of the series. I was also amused with the part where Frank was gifted a set of cufflinks with one letter of his initials in each piece, but I am digressing.

Pain and failure have a way of teaching us lessons and storing them in our long-term memory. Even if we try to forget, failure is coded into how we behave going forward. It is nature's way.

As they say: once bitten, twice shy.

I know we should learn from the mistakes of others. That works too, to some extent, but the warning does not go deep as there is no pain. Sadly, people forget and they are soon off to the wrong path. And that is when they finally learn.

Related to pain somewhat is the concept of "hunger." When you do not have enough, when you don't have a plan B, you are always reminded of how hard you might fall and never recover. Staring into the abyss is a good teacher.

A local tycoon put it in a practical way: errors of commission versus errors of omission.

Long before talking about failure became fashionable, he told me that he does not punish his people for making mistakes while initiating or acting. But he gets mad when they do not take action.

Painfully clear.

Customer Experience Moments of Truth

The best test for our products and services is when there is an emergency or problem. How we respond can win long-term loyalty, or lose a customer. That is why these are referred to as Moments of Truth.

What do we do when:

There is fraud
A failed remittance
Disapproved card purchase
A lost card or undelivered card
No cash dispensed in ATM
When the system slows down or dies…

We need to be ready whenever these happen.

Designing and building a delightful customer experience is an ongoing exercise. Avoiding and monitoring of errors is a priority for us. We also have to keep auditing the experience because there is always some potential for unknown unknowns.

Putting solutions in the mobile app is a good first step. Second, we need to ensure our call center agents are equipped to handle such types of inquiries to reduce customer anxiety. Third, we scan social media for negative feedback and firm up our response.

We cannot always fully trust outsourced providers, especially as the demand for tech and logistic services has ballooned and our providers are stretched thin. They have their own training and recruitment issues. We need to independently check for service quality on a regular basis.

In the end, service culture makes the biggest difference. This is difficult in an environment where a 12% minimum employee turnover is the norm. Managers have to pay better attention and be more creative in hiring, including building a factory training new employees and retaining them.

Customer Complaint is Free Consultation, with Feelings

Negative feedback is a gift, my friend Grace who runs a thriving digital company shared with me yesterday. Most customers, when unhappy, will just drop and forget you. At least some decide to make the effort of writing. Research suggests that every complaint we receive represents between five and ten unsatisfied customers.

I agree.

Some customers rant on social media. They may not always paint a fair picture, and we are put in a bad light.

It stings, but it shows you your blind spots. It is an opportunity to improve on your product. Best of all, you have a golden chance to convince even an angry customer to stick with you, provided you respond quickly and respectfully.

It is not easy, I admit. It can come with an angry tone, may be condescending, or might be downright insulting. Still, when you put yourself in the client's context, it is easier to swallow.

There are rare instances when the client is entirely unreasonable, or they bully our staff. They cross the line. That is a different story. I become protective of our employees whenever that happens.

Of course, I am happy when clients compliment us on our services. Just the same, I ask them to help us by giving ideas for improvement. They usually have something to say. Like, "Bank C has this really interesting product feature." That is a gift as well.

In the Asian setting, it is harder to solicit negative feedback, but you can always put it in a constructive context.

Resilience

After having seen the 1997 Asian Crisis, the GFC, and recently COVID, I have realized this: crisis brings out the best in people.

I see evidence of commitment, clarity, and courage.

- Commitment to do what it takes despite constraints, diligently looking for solutions and not making excuses.
- Clarity of thinking — ability to process more information under stress and make better decisions.
- Courage to transform the business as usual, cut costs, and exploit new opportunities. Manage the bad, but go after the good.

Sadly, I also see the flipside: inability to act, sense of loss, and refusal to change.

Like dealing with failure, we learn from each crisis and try our best to make the lessons a permanent part of our new improved selves. The word used to describe that is "resilience," as if it is a new thing. In fact, it kind of actually is.

Resilience comes from a Latin word that means "leap back." It was once used to describe the ability of materials to regain its original form. We used the word as a technical term in physics laboratories in 1980 when we stressed metal wires. As we added weights, the copper wire lengthened. As we gradually removed the load, the wire returned to the original measure. It was only in the last 50 years when the term started applying to people and, fairly recently, to organizations.

The difference between metal and people is that people don't just recover, they can grow and get better.

”

People do not realize their full potential until they challenge themselves.

Chapter Eight

Aim to Outperform

I know, people always say "underpromise but outperform." My problem with this is that goals become compromised downwards to ensure they are met. The risk is the achievement of a mediocre objective.

I prefer that my teams be reasonably aggressive, and raise the bar. People do not realize their full potential until they challenge themselves. The wonderful thing about this is, even if they fall short initially, they will know how to do better in the next round.

Set Goals That Inspire

The old formula for setting objectives demanded that they be specific, measurable, achievable, relevant, and timebound. I learned this as a new manager.

Over time, I realized this was not enough. It needed a boost, a powerful one, something that motivates.

A goal should be one that inspires. Not just a number. It should represent something employees can be emotionally attached to, be proud of. Something that, when achieved, needs no further financial reward.

For the bank, the slogan #fightto5 stood for bringing back the bank to its industry position in the past. It was something the employees felt very strongly about.

On the other hand, it is perilous when the leader and team fall in love with a goal that is not rooted in reality.

What is needed is an honest reality check that rationally evaluates the gap between the present situation and the goal. One way to do this is to look at others who accomplished similar objectives and find out what resources, skills, and new competencies are required.

And "achievability" should also be chopped into timebound steps so that the goal does not overwhelm. For example, an ambitious sales target can be reduced to a number of daily proposals so that they appear attainable and can be managed.

Finally, when measuring, it has to be compared with competitors. Beating the budget while underperforming the industry does not make me happy. On the other hand, going below budget but outdoing competition should be rewarded.

When Salespeople Don't Sell

The usual methods of motivation are sales incentives, promotions, and commissions. These work.

The least obvious but most basic way, which people often overlook, is to provide a good product that compares favorably against other brands and services.

New products will be viewed with suspicion. It may take some courage for the first person to sell them. Why? Because every salesperson will protect his/her existing relationships with clients. A product failure will put relationships at risk.

In the finance industry, this is crucial. A single bad experience can end a customer relationship. For example, if a rich depositor is denied a new credit card, or if the card takes long to be delivered, it is the relationship manager's role to appease the customer.

What this means is that salespeople need to "buy" the product first before they start selling it. They have to believe. Otherwise they censor, and will make excuses.

This is probably why product launches have a "preachy" feeling about them. They are emotional as they are rational.

One of the less dramatic ways to win salespeople over is to let them play around with the product whenever possible. Test drive the new car. If it is an app, make them try it out first so they feel comfortable and can suggest improvements. Another way is to get inputs from them when redesigning existing products or developing new ones. They have to "own" it to some extent.

In the end, if they don't believe, they won't sell.

The Peril in Performance Appraisals

Trust grows from fairness and care when doing performance appraisals. By being objective, transparent, and consistent, the leader avoids any semblance of bias or favoritism. An employee will welcome your feedback if he/she knows you sincerely care, that this is not just a routine that is mandated by the company.

Whenever possible, get to know your employee better. Invest in what I would like to call "relationship capital." Help the employee build a career. By spending time discussing how an individual can improve and how the person's career can progress, the leader encourages trust and retention.

To remove arbitrariness, try to be quantitative with goals. This will allow you to compare performance across the team.

Over many workshops on managing, I have been taught how to deliver the not-so-good part of the appraisal. There was even this "sandwich" approach where negative feedback was relayed between two goods. Or start with three good ones, and then three points for improvement.

I honestly do not remember anymore. Now, I prefer to discuss performance many times over the year. The year-end meeting should not have any surprises.

There is more. Appraisals should put a premium on extraordinary performance. A performance appraisal needs to distinguish those who just meet targets or match industry records, versus those who commit to higher goals and dare to outperform.

As I keep reminding my leaders, I prefer to fall short of an aggressive but well-thought objective, than to achieve an average aim.

Mind Over Matter

Expensive employees do not necessarily have the highest salaries. Ironically, many of those with high salaries are mathematically the cheapest.

Why? Measure expense relative to value delivered. Let me simplify. For example, a mid-salaried employee paid a unit of 1 may deliver an output of 5. A top-performing peer paid 2x may have an output of 20. The cost for the first is 0.2 and for the second is 0.1. Half. The all-in cost of the second employee is even better if you add office space and other overhead, like rent and depreciation.

Productivity is what matters. I have seen this often in sales functions where performance can be quantified.

What to do?

The first is a reminder that leaders have to intervene early on to set employees up for success. Training and tools can raise productivity. It is best to inculcate correct behavior at the start.

Second, increase variable compensation, meaning be more commission-based. Output beyond the norm or budget should be given extra rewards based on a formula. Otherwise top employees may not feel properly valued, and will search for alternative employment offers.

Finally, track results. I learned this in elementary school when we had newspaper drives. Next to the principal's office was a set of colored bars that represented how many newspapers each class had gathered. If you were ahead, everyone knew. If you were sleeping, everyone knew as well. No one wanted to be the last.

If you and others look at the scoreboard frequently enough, it moves faster. It is not telekinesis. Thankfully, it is human nature.

Heir and Spare: Succession Planning

One obligation that some leaders forget, even deliberately ignore, is the issue of succession. Leaders are not princes of the universe. They are stewards of their organizations and have to make sure their companies continue to flourish when they pass the baton to whoever comes next in line.

It is common practice to identify at least two potential successors for critical roles. Each candidate is assessed for readiness, and a timeline for career development is set.

It becomes problematic when no candidates are found. Then we scrounge the market for talented individuals and find that they are often already spoken for.

I pay special attention to these high-potential officers. They take a disproportionate amount of time from me. I know them personally.

My preference is that succession planning starts with the hiring of high-caliber talent into junior or mid-officer levels. We have to think — can this young man/woman lead a big group or even this company someday? Then we train and rotate them across the organization.

This has to be well-organized and properly tracked because this is mission critical, a must have. Compensation may even be structured in a way that encourages high-potentials to stay.

From these hires will rise future leaders. We have to accept that we will lose some, but many will stay because they have something to look forward to. The ones we lose will still be our allies.

Succession planning that is sustainable takes at least a decade or more. It is best to start early.

Give Specialists a Generalist View

Employees in highly skilled roles are paid more than the usual rate for the same rank in other parts of the organization. This is because there is less supply of the specific skill in the marketplace. Data science is the most recent example.

For the lucky employee, he/she gets to enjoy the perks obviously, but will still sometimes think what his/her market value is outside the organization. Leaders need to be mindful of that.

There is a downside, however. The high pay continues as long as the person specializes in the current role, and will likely miss the chance to work in other positions. To me, this is the more serious issue. A golden handcuff.

The career progression needs to move to other parts of the company to complete the person's preparation for senior positions, and build an internal network. This calls for a new type of training that enables specialists to learn more about the company while full-time in their current roles.

In the bank, we launched a part-time management training program that focuses on:

Treasury
Operations
Products
Governance
Underwriting and
i**N**novation.

It is always nice to brand programs with exciting acronyms to increase awareness and encourage applications. Figuring out names takes time. I sure do hope this new one will soar and be deserving of its name.

Flat or Fat

I have been to organizations which are very flat, and to others where there are seniors who literally manage managers who also manage managers.

I immediately see it as an opportunity to cut fat. Layers who do not have customer or production responsibility tend to ask for information, organize it for presentations, and gather more information again. The officers below them end up putting together data unnecessarily. And wastefully. Until they decide to leave because the effort is unproductive and not career-enhancing.

Too many chiefs, too few warriors. Too many information brokers and too few doers.

A major international bank went on a major reorganization recently. It used to be well-known for its matrix organization. This meant having two (or three) supervisors. They stopped the practice and are now lean.

Flat organizations often have only one full-time manager in each group or division. He/she is responsible for financial targets, and also goes on the road to generate revenues and mentor younger officers. And between four and seven direct reports, although this has to be properly evaluated.

When we have seniors who only have two direct reports, I think no further evaluation is required unless the seniors themselves are "doers" most of the time and only part-time managers. Two is too few.

Finally, I believe that decisions should be pushed down to the most junior competent level. It is like saying that the commander in the field knows the terrain better and should be given authority. Resist the urge to second guess. If what is at stake is not considerable anyway, use it to test the juniors.

Sales Rallies

One Saturday, we were in the office for rallies of two business groups. As you know, these rah-rah sessions are usually held at the start of the year to celebrate the previous year's successes, award top performers, set the tone for the coming year, brainstorm about strategy, and define priorities.

I am usually invited to speak. I do not waste the chance to address entire groups.

It is a good time to remind them that they are stars. Tell them how and where they did well. Like saying a sincere "thank you," I explain why I am grateful in specific terms. It is an opportunity to learn from the recent past. Even if we take a victory lap, we need to recognize areas where we can do better, without sounding like a kill-joy. We highlight personal achievement, with a bit of humor at the top performer's expense.

In the first session, we discussed how to improve customer service. We have done much in this area, 10 action points, and we have been rewarded with the number one rating in the customer service survey for commercial banks. This activity was more a reminder on how to deal with customer complaints, why those complaints are an opportunity to delight, and the need to be authentic and avoid sounding scripted.

The second group later that afternoon was more of a competitive strategy session. How do we reposition our existing product bundles to persuade customers of other banks to switch to us? We need to make a case based on pain points with their existing providers, and the comparative benefits from our offerings.

Sales rallies should be relevant. It should address the group's priorities.

The downside of these sessions is, when adrenaline dissipates, (satisfied) sleepiness sets in.

Exponential Human Resources

I swear there was a time in the '80s and '90s when I was convinced HR's objective was to keep the salary expense as low as possible. I also thought they had the strictest level of approvals. Thankfully, this changed.

Gone are the days when HR simply meant payroll and benefits. Organizational development and cultural transformation are now what make the biggest difference. The new HR in the 2000s is a strategic partner of business groups. It is instrumental in cultural renewal as we turbo up digital transformation, customer obsession, and employee upskilling. In fact, organizations that harness HR's capabilities are ahead of those that do not.

This demands that HR folks learn the whys and hows of the company's business strategy. An HR pro needs to be familiar with AI and data science, for example. An HR officer should also be a digital banker.

Nowadays, employee branding is imperative as companies compete for talent. Training programs now take in engineers and scientists, and HR has to turn them into bankers. HR has to digitally market for recruitment.

That is probably why I agreed to speak at the People Management Annual Convention three times in the last three years. And I always try my best to accommodate requests to speak to our HR colleagues. This is because I believe that they have a multiplier, even exponential effect on the morale, productivity, and innovation skills of the organization.

To win, our people have to be the best versions of themselves. I rely on HR to make this happen. They give me leverage.

And as Archimedes once declared: "Give me a place to stand, and a lever long enough, and I will move the world."

The Risk of Promoting Top Performers to Management Roles

The best performers, often highest rated, are promoted fast until they get the chance to become managers. This is defensible because their peers probably respect their status, and performance should always be part of the consideration anyway. Promoting second-stringers ahead of the best performers is harder to justify.

Unfortunately, this is also when problems start. Leading a team requires a set of skills quite different from being a superstar individual contributor. Leading needs EQ, to put it briefly. It has to be learned.

Companies I have worked for addressed this through training programs. I remember going through New Manager Training that dealt with basic things like performance appraisals and setting smart goals. An example is the bank's middle management development program for division heads that focus on soft skills.

Another good practice is to assess a potential manager's leadership skills through projects, collaboration with other groups, and other activities. In all these interactions, the officer's supervisor is able to assess potential for more senior roles.

Finally, those labeled high-potential officers should be assigned mentors early on, and be guided when they finally assume management positions.

It is good that companies now make it a point to equip the best performers and make them ready for leadership roles.

Why Employees Leave

My HR mentor in Citibank once explained to me that over 90% of employees who quit their companies did so because they did not see their careers developing in the coming years. There were, of course, other reasons like horrible bosses and low pay.

I always get reminded of Maslow's hierarchy of needs when analyzing these types of issues, coupled with evaluation of actual situations. For example, when a young employee is the breadwinner of his/her family, pay becomes a primary consideration, and giving a competitive package is the solution.

The next question I ask is if the employee has a best friend at work. I learned from a Gallup material (which they have written extensively on) that having a best friend is key to employee engagement. Whenever I mentor, I ask this question to check whether my mentee's social needs are being met. The answers are often telling.

Of course, there were times when I wanted to leave Citi. The first was when I thought I was given a second-class job (I was very wrong). The second was when I had an undesirable boss. The camaraderie of the team convinced me to stay.

As a new manager in the '90s, I benefited from a performance appraisal process which required me to identify each employee's areas for improvement, and to write a career development plan. Over the years, this has become the focal point of my appraisal discussions for middle management layers.

The discussions don't have to be formal. These can also be covered during informal one-on-one sessions.

Finally, I have to stress that the annual appraisal process has to be taken seriously, and not simply be a form-filling exercise. To me, that is how to retain our best employees.

Medals for All, Manifest!

I have kept all my medals since Grade 1. They still look okay even if they are half-a-century old.

In 1980, when I was graduating from high school, the principal faced budgetary constraints and unilaterally decided to forgo giving the best-in-subject awards. At least five medals vanished into thin air. In fact, all the medals awarded came free from external sources.

In the '90s, I began noticing that kindergarten graduates were wearing togas with several medals dangling around their necks. Some got the awards for having the best smile. I could have won that, too. They looked happy; good for them and their parents.

Then in 2002, I joined my first 10-kilometer run in Singapore. They gave all finishers a medal. The other subsequent races gave certificates. That was then a huge deal for me. I went on and ran longer. My collection grew. The certificates lost novelty over time but I kept running for over a decade.

Maybe the real reward, apart from endorphins, was shopping for smaller-sized clothes that followed. I was never that fit or healthy ever in my life. The double chin shrank.

Admittedly, there was a time when I wasn't sure whether I deserved the medal. I definitely ran a total of 20 kilometers every week for many months just to prepare, but I was far from being a top competitor. Maybe going slightly uphill from Tanglin to the Botanic Gardens every week deserves some recognition. At least I did not get it just for showing up. I got it as a memento for finishing, for real effort.

It is not the same as a participation medal, one that is given simply for joining events, although some people do not see any difference.

There is a huge debate about participation medals. The pros claim that it encourages kids to join various activities and teaches camaraderie. Critics insist that it gives a false sense of achievement, and deprives children (and adults) the lesson of resilience that failure teaches.

There has to be balance, I think. Do not give a medal just for showing up. Give only when commendable tasks are completed at a satisfactory level. And then promote competition and highlight performance that clearly stands out, where only the best gets recognized.

Recently, I learned a new millennial word — "manifest." When a branch manager saw his colleague win the Best Branch Award last year, he manifested to himself that he will get it this year. He did! The same thing happened to the young man who won Best in Bancassurance. He also manifested.

I don't know how many told themselves they were going to win it. I suspect at least 100 manifested.

It is important to reward the troops for meeting their targets, but even more crucial to inspire them to set their aims higher and be the one onstage. When they don't get it, they have the next year to make a go at it again. Despite the prevalence of participation awards, my teammates still aspire to reach the very top.

Manifest that!

”

To win, our people have to be the best versions of themselves.

Part Three

Be a Digital Advocate

”

Productive employees tend to become happy employees, and happy employees lead to delighted customers.

Chapter Nine

Embrace Data Science and AI

I always try to spend an hour with the data science team several times a year to discuss the bank's strategy and action plans. I challenge them to figure out ways analytics and AI can assist in doing banking more effectively. I'd like to think that this is the reason why they understand our direction and how they can play an active part.

For CEOs and leaders wanting to engage data scientists, I strongly suggest that you immerse yourselves in their world by actually taking formal data science courses.

Five Data Scientists

I spent four hours with five highly qualified individuals whose careers were wholly or partially focused on data science, automation, and artificial intelligence. This was what I learned:

1. Data scientists cannot succeed in environments where business leaders are unaware of how analytics tools can help businesses. An intro course on data and AI should now be a minimum requirement. Stop using data scientists for simple MIS (management information system) needs. They can do much more.

2. One of the best ways to turn businesses into believers is to show how data is transforming other industries. I remember being blown away 10 years ago by how casinos in the US used analytics as a tool for customer engagement. I couldn't wait to see how I could apply this in my own field.

3. Data scientists tend to be introverted. They need to build friendships across various parts of the company. These friendships can informally build teamwork, especially if the formal structure is not progressive.

4. Data scientists look for meaning, for relevance in their work. They need to feel that they are part of the bigger community and that they understand the big picture. Don't give them token projects. Put them where they can contribute to revenue generation, like in sales and marketing.

5. Domain expertise, like gaining professional certifications in investment management, is an excellent way by which data scientists can differentiate themselves. I have met data pros who are experts in supply chain, chemical engineering, renewables. I suggested that they also study in-depth the industry that their companies belong to, and learn about corporate strategy.

Data, AI, and CX

I was invited to join a group of speakers and industry experts to discuss how innovation can radically transform customer experience. The audience consisted mostly of bankers.

In my 15-minute presentation, I highlighted how our bank made the bet five years ago on RPA (robotic process automation), AI, and data science, and how it made our salespeople and other employees far more productive. Every morning, thanks to data science, all our branches receive a customized report that identifies actionable customer trends and opportunities.

We have over 50 AI models that have significantly improved lead generation in our sales channels. We put together a matrix of credit scores and high-propensity grades generated by analytics, and our salespeople use this as their primary calling list. Sales directors track activity based on the list.

By predicting customer behavior in repayment, purchase, next-best offer, and even email habits, we optimized resources. By grouping similar customers together based on behavior and other parameters, we created personas for whom we tailored relevant offers.

Never underestimate the power of productivity in driving up morale among the salespeople. Productive employees tend to become happy employees, and happy employees lead to delighted customers.

However, tech alone won't work. CX (customer experience) has to be ingrained in the company's culture. In our case, one practice is to deep dive into top customer complaints every month, identifying root causes and brainstorming together to fix those problems. Data analytics is part of this process.

Data, Hypothesis, Gut Feel, Biases

I hear the word "hypothesis" more often now, as if we are in a science class. When we have a tentative idea about a problem or opportunity, we check the data first to see if we can disprove our initial thoughts. This often leads to new insights.

The hypothesis may be based on previous experience, even gut feel.

There was a time when decisions were made on gut feel alone by experienced leaders. It is, anyway, informal data gathered over many years of experience, through good times and bad.

The thing is, experienced individuals disagree, although in our team this is done in a healthy manner with a bit of banter. I have found that backgrounds matter. We have biases we are unaware of. We often take for granted that our previous jobs had different resources, strengths, markets, and other parameters.

We bring all our pasts, our ways of thinking, into our current roles.

This is actually good because the discussion is enriched by diversity. And I have found it enlightening when I ask myself (and colleagues) why we think a certain way. Does my Citi DNA influence my decisions? Good thing we have HSBC, Maybank, and other "histories" thrown into the mix.

For example, bankers that come from transaction banking powerhouses tend to use cash management as a leading product. Those who don't might use credit instead. It is also useful to check where our competitors learned their trade. It will explain their preferred strategies. I am happiest and most relieved whenever hypotheses are proven wrong, because that means traditional practices no longer hold true.

Data Science in a Vacuum

There are, thankfully, more data scientists nowadays compared to five years ago when we started establishing our team. It has helped that physicists, mathematicians, and engineers have jumped in and added to the supply of talent.

Schools like AIM have offered programs that launched careers of young people from various backgrounds. The new part-time program makes this even more accessible.

So what's next?

A data science team cannot exist in a vacuum. It needs to be part of an ecosystem where business leaders understand and appreciate how analytics can drive value, and where data scientists are pulled in to be part of strategy and business discussions as partners.

The biggest stumbling block is that businesses may think of the analytics team as just MIS on steroids. That would be a disaster, on steroids, a costly mistake.

During meetings with my data scientists, I had several "aha!" moments when I found insights I never thought of before. Sometimes they were counter-intuitive.

This only happens when the team is very much a part of business strategy, and not simply an MIS source.

My wish is that we have more scientists who have domain expertise in other parts of the bank (or other parts of the company). This will happen when bankers in treasury, sales, and lending pursue graduate programs in data science. This has already started to happen.

Artificial Intelligence and Judas

AI has benefited us in ways I did not imagine six years ago. Even then, I expected it was going to radically transform banking. Now, it has proven incredibly powerful in increasing employee productivity and elevating customer experience.

I am relieved that we chose AI as our priority over the other digital tools that were available. Otherwise, we would be playing catch-up today. For instance, AI enables us to predict a customer's propensity to take a car loan. And a second car loan which I found quite amusing as it negated our preconceived notions on the timing. This has been of major interest to me. I am curious as to what we will discover next.

What bank product will he/she purchase next? What will be his/her payment behavior?

And we do credit scoring which quickens the decision process. That's just for starters.

In the Philippines, the most popular sign in jeepneys is "God knows Judas not pay," with the "J" pronounced as "H." "Hudas" sounds like "who does." I often joke that, with AI, you can avoid lending to Judas ahead of time.

We are now experimenting with GenAI (generative AI). Beyond having a capable analytics/AI team, it is important to collaborate with like-minded organizations to accelerate adoption.

If you add up all the applications in sales, fraud management, and risk management alone, it is easy to believe that AI can increase productivity by 50% in the future.

Mathematically Describing Human Behavior

Back in the '80s, I enjoyed explaining why a tennis ball drops early in a well-executed forehand. And why windows open with a bang during typhoons, seemingly defying reason. These examples make fluid mechanics more interesting to learn.

Physics, after all, describes how nature behaves. There were many such cases we used to take the boredom and fear out of a dreadful required subject. (Don't forget to add sailing against the wind!)

I sometimes think I studied physics decades too early. When I graduated, there were few opportunities outside the academe. The laser lab was the coolest thing then. Now, many clinics have lasers. In the '90s, physics was employed to predict how financial markets worked. It wasn't always perfectly done, but the approximation was scary and phenomenal. No wonder we had physicists, engineers, and mathematicians in my derivative sales and structuring team at Citi. We had more in risk management. It felt like we had our own faculty that could grant degrees.

Our customers were quantitative fund managers with similar academic backgrounds. They still exist and have more powerful computer tools.

Now, physicists still lurk in trading rooms globally, but the younger ones have migrated to data analytics where the work is more exciting.

My senior data scientist (she has a double PhD in physics and data science) who recently joined us after doing research on smart cities explained that even though human behavior is the most difficult to model, physics skills are now being used to improve people's lives.

I agree.

Why Do Chemical Engineers Do Well in Data Science?

I have been asking this question many times, as I have seen a significant number of chemical engineering majors in data science resumes (after stats and physics). I initially thought this might be because computer/electrical majors have gravitated towards hardware or coding.

I have noticed a similar trend in manufacturing engineering. I currently mentor three ChEs. The first is currently still in university but leaning towards data science. The second heads data analytics in an insurance company. The third chose to establish himself in renewable energy. And all three manufacturing engineers I meet regularly are hard-core data scientists.

I met Colin Christie who studied chemical engineering in Berkeley, and has been the driving force of the local analytics and AI association. For many minutes, we were finishing each other's sentences, and then I posed the question.

He reasoned that after studying organic, inorganic, and other basic chemistry in the early years, the subjects shift to systems, the operation of manufacturing plants, and how to convert raw material inventory into finished products. This logic obviously applies to manufacturing engineering as well.

The type of thinking that goes on for at least three years is similar to that required in the new field of data science. The quantitative skills and the use of analytical tools are, of course, already a given.

I asked the younger ones and they independently declared the same reason.

”

I am happiest and most relieved whenever hypotheses are proven wrong, because that means traditional practices no longer hold true.

”

Complaints and compliments are the basis for future development.

Chapter Ten

Accelerate Digital Adoption

Beyond the technical aspects, the digital leader is first an evangelist.

A digital transformation exercise demands a massive amount of investment in technology and people. The leader needs to persuade the board and other stakeholders to support the required capital outlay by presenting a credible transformation plan that will include building new business models, expense reductions, and future revenue streams.

Then the leader has to make it happen. But he can only do this through the support and hard work of all employees.

The Digital Leader

As digital transformation will affect hundreds and thousands of jobs, the leader must go to town halls explaining to groups how their businesses will be affected, the significant upside for the company, and the career growth prospects for those who upskill.

Culture will need to change into one that is agile, customer-obsessed, and collaborative. The leader will work with HR on cultural transformation initiatives, and celebrate small victories achieved by new projects manned by cross-functional teams, while ensuring these projects are focused on real customer pain points.

The leader will convince a new type of employees — data scientists, engineers, coders — who do not fit the traditional mold to join the company, and then make them feel welcome.

Given finite resources, the leader has to choose alternatives and opportunities that are consistent with the digital business strategy. Priority has to be given to scalable products rather than those with limited potential.

Not everything will go as planned. The leader will keep the energy level high, remind everyone that failure is part of the process as long as we quickly learn from it, and strive to get better.

It turns out that, at the top of the company, soft skills are more important than technical skills. But a leader who is familiar with digital and data tools can better interact with the technology side of the company. I refrain from prescribing what companies should look for in their new CEOs. That is not my intention. However, we should recognize that we are at a Darwinian point in history where those who adapt to change will survive and thrive.

The Digital Imperative

Our way of life as consumers has radically evolved. I still enjoy going to Kinokuniya, but I can order books online. We get our ride through the Grab app. We carry little cash, preferring digital payments. Few will disagree that digital transformation is important. However, let me state three reasons why, so it is clear that digitalization is not just for show. It is actually existential.

1. Better customer experience, personalized — it radically improves CX as buyers can now use their phones to access products without leaving their homes, 24/7. Offerings can be personalized using data and AI in terms of product features, selling approach, and engagement. When CX is superior to that of competition, sales volume increases.

2. Cheaper to deliver — online and mobile channels are substantially cheaper on a marginal cost per transaction basis once the platforms are built. No need for physical outlets. Middle and back offices can also be automated, thus reducing error, opex, and turnaround time. There is room for outsourcing and rapidly scaling technology capacity.

3. Quicker product launches — once agile culture and collaboration are ingrained in the company, time-to-market is much faster compared to the old methods of product development. Innovation is customer-focused. This, however, demands continuous improvement and attention to customer complaints.

When executed judiciously, all these result in business growth, good financials, favorable industry reputation, and better employee morale.

The Leader as a Data Science Enthusiast

There are minimum requirements from a technical standpoint. A digital leader needs to establish familiarity with digital tools, especially how they can be utilized for his/her business.

He/she does not have to know how to code (I am not sure if my antiquated coding skills are still useful), but previous programming experience enables the leader to relate to non-traditional employees. The leader also does not have to be an engineer, a quant, or scientist. Or a physicist. He just needs to be able to understand the new tools, and engage in open discussions with the technical experts.

For example, data science, analytics, and AI. Apart from data scientists, heavy-duty modelers, machine learning engineers, campaign analysts, and data engineers, there is the business analyst function lodged between data science and the business. This role understands both sides very well and is able to articulate the business objective and how data science can potentially help. It is a big plus if the digital leader is trained to do this task.

There are online courses and short programs that will allow leaders to quickly dive into this territory. I recommend the Johns Hopkins Executive Data Science course, the one offered by Columbia, and Professor Andrew Ng's various YouTube videos and courses on AI.

The leader also has to ensure that the data scientists live in an ecosystem that is convinced of the power of analytics in radically cutting down turnaround time, personalizing offerings, and anticipating customer behavior.

And decisions should start to be driven by data and experimentation. Data can confirm gut feel.

The Leader as an Automation Sponsor

Together with data and AI, some knowledge of automation will be very useful.

Robotic process automation has proven effective in taking over menial, manual, repetitive, and error-prone tasks, and completing them instantaneously. This results in sharp reductions in turnaround time, enhanced employee experience, and fewer errors.

There are companies that help set up RPA schemes for clients. I was lucky my own team already had experience migrating branch processes to bots. After installing the bots, we were able to save hundreds of headcount that we later shifted to sales roles.

Migrating manual processes from counters and contact centers to the mobile app leads to significant cost savings. For example, time deposits, foreign exchange, investment transactions, payments, balance inquiries, and many more are now accessible through bank mobile apps.

Actually, much of the investment can be justified by the reduction of physical channels and the lesser need for human intervention. As you know, physical channels are very expensive to run, and manpower is between 30% and 40% of bank opex.

Over time, the percentage of transactions done digitally, or away from the bank counters, should materially rise. We are already seeing an almost flat trend in over-the-counter transactions.

From Marketing to Digital Marketing

Speaking of sales, digital marketing is so vastly different from traditional marketing that they even have their own professional certification process. A branch of data science works with digital marketing to create social media campaigns and analyze their effectiveness.

When was the last time you watched TV? You are probably on Facebook or Instagram a thousand times more. Research says consumers tend to distrust conventional ads and would rather listen to friends and family and influencers on social media. Marketing has to keep an eye on all these. Thankfully, sentiment can now be tracked using AI.

Optimize your digital assets for searches so you don't get buried (meaning hardly ever seen during a search). Pay for keywords so your ads show up first on social media. Measure click-throughs and bounces, and time spent on your websites. Determine the best time to send marketing emails by studying client email behavior. This is a science in itself. Marketing has become quite quantitative and I am bombarded with numbers during marketing discussions.

Just recently, I watched a digital marketing expert explain why she needed to send a similar message in five different formats across several digital channels when selling skincare products. That was pretty amazing. I thought all along that sending more than two messages would be considered annoying.

I was fortunate to have attended classes leading to a Digital Marketing Professional certification, and took a Wharton Online course as I found the quantitative marketing section appealing. But you have to keep engaging with practitioners because this battleground is getting more sophisticated.

Internet Banks in 2009 versus Today's Digital Lenders

Thirteen years ago, as I was about to take on my first CEO job, I picked up several books to brush up on topics I was not that familiar with. The one that got my attention was banking technology, and the subject I thought most about was internet banking.

I remember what it said: internet banks paid higher interest rates and spent more for advertising. And charged lower for loans to encourage borrowers to choose the bank. The result was thin margins. There was also a psychological hurdle as customers looked for physical branches to go to in case they had problems.

There was marginal success back then. Compared to present standards, the tech infrastructure then was vastly inferior in terms of speed, size, and storage. Customer behavior and demographics also mattered a great deal. Most people back then grew up banking over the counter compared to today's digital natives who don't.

Now, digital banks have better technology, favorable customer behavior, and even friendly regulations. Unfortunately, according to Boston Consulting Group, only 5% are profitable.

The ones who are doing well are generally attached to a group or owner that already has a set of customers, data from those customers, a well-known and trusted brand, an established record in technology, and deep, deep pockets. You can argue that, for groups with promising digital banks, the banking part is simply a new, adjacent business to their existing portfolio.

Even so, the revenue source, usually loans, needs to be established. Unless a reliable credit bureau exists, there will be a higher degree of dependence on existing customer data. Finally, loans need to be collected from borrowers. You cannot assume reliance on the goodness of their hearts, otherwise cost of credit will cripple the business.

Agile Methodology Demands CX

When new digital products are launched, they are far from perfect, but they can fix the customer pain point. They may also be better than current alternative solutions, or even be the only solution. They work in a "minimum viable" way.

The new product is analogous to a hypothesis, but like the scientific method, this hypothesis is tested with the customer. Sometimes we discover that our customers use our product differently (in a good way) from what we had intended. Complaints and compliments are the basis for future development. This is why our monthly CX Council meetings at the bank are crucial as we uncover root causes and brainstorm fixes. The product squads/teams meet even more frequently.

When I started as a banker, new product launches had to be thoroughly vetted and documented. This took long to accomplish. There was also little patience for error or failure. Now, agility and resilience are the accepted values. This is fine because for new product solutions, we do not have the luxury of time and resources. We do not even know what "perfect" is!

This was one of the points I stressed during my presentation one Thursday to customer experience officers (CXOs). You start with a scooter to move from point A to point B, but you keep rebuilding while moving until maybe you have something that looks like a car.

I only had 15 minutes to deliver my talk and tried to pack as much into the slides before going back to the glass of Mount Gay Rum from Barbados. As I will mention again in another chapter, that was the first drink Daniel Craig ordered as James Bond. This fact is too notable to mention just once.

Netflix and My Barbershop

Our customers no longer compare banks against each other. Their standards are now based on the best companies and impeccable services they have ever experienced.

Take for example CX. I have read many articles that propose Netflix as the new standard for customer experience. By using AI and whatever else, the choices posed are stimulating compared to the two other competing providers. (I still subscribed to others because one carried *Dune* and the other *Game of Thrones*; content is still king.)

When we launched the new version of our mobile app, it immediately got compared with the old app that customers were already used to. (Talk about competing with your old self!) I think we don't have to go very far. My barbershop is a great example of CX. BackAlley is linked to an app that allows you to set an appointment which you can easily change. When you get in, you see books, coffee, and beer.

The staff are efficient and they don't smother you with chorales of greetings. I am received with a friendly smile. They are punctual, polite, and focused on their tasks. Everyone is relaxed and quiet. Oftentimes, I am dozing off into dreamland.

I don't own the place, but I feel like it is mine.

One realization: the more digital the world has evolved, the more relevant face-to-face has become.

Great Design

I have always been fascinated with bridges, marveling at how engineering and design together can produce something beautiful. The third Cebu bridge, for example, is not simply a means to cross the Mactan Channel; it is the city's new symbol.

I feel the same way about some buildings, like the lobby of RCBC Plaza or the former Citi Tower in Hong Kong, often stopping and looking up, admiring the ambience. And the Mactan Airport makes you wonder why similar facilities in the country don't look a third as pretty.

I am inspired when in Madrid's airport. The mix of yellow and wood in Barajas is simply lovely to stare at. I don't mind if my flight is delayed a bit. Design. It is about design.

Before diving into my current job, I spent a week trying to understand the layout of apps and websites. Our class of 20 suffered through concepts with the goal of passing the UX Certification from the British Computer Society. Over half the class hurdled the exams. I learned and passed, but I still did not have the "answer."

Finally, I had the great fortune of listening to the Chief Designer of Montblanc. When he uttered the simple phrase "beautiful and useful," I knew I was satisfied. The app has to be beautiful and useful.

I have kept repeating those words, even as I still prefer my stainless steel Cross pen.

Recently, the CEO of Rockwell showed me around their recent developments. I decided to change "beautiful" to "gorgeous."

Love at First Call

Nobody likes to dial the call center. I evade it the same way I steer clear of visits to the dentist. I even like to define a call center as a place that does not answer calls. Everyone, except maybe the call center employees, agree. How do we get better?

First, we avoid calls and try to move them to the mobile channel and the chatbot. Like balance information, which is now often on the landing page in bank mobile apps. For example, RCBC was the first local bank that enabled customers to convert card purchases into installments in just a few clicks. This radically cut down call-ins.

Second, every month we do a root cause analysis of the bulk of the calls/emails/posts so that these are avoided going forward. The solution is often creative and the result of a collaborative brainstorming session. We also track the number of dropped calls, waiting time, and the number of minutes per call. We compare the stats with industry standards.

But the metric I like the most is first call resolution, which literally means the percentage of calls immediately solved without any subsequent conversations. This requires giving the agents a level of authority to approve certain accommodations.

I often test our capabilities by sometimes calling. When they ask for my name, I give it. Our agents, being outsourced, do not know who I am. This is work in progress, and needs appropriate focus. The main lesson here is the need to manage down anxiety levels of everyone, including that of our employees.

Bridgital

What is bridgital?

We invented this word to describe digital tools that still entertain cash and check usage in processes that are one or two steps away from being fully digital. It is a compromise.

For example, a cash cube machine solution which accepts cash deposits in the client's premises for same-day credit. A collection service picks up the cash later.

Another is a check scanning machine that does not require checks to be brought to the bank in time for clearing. The customers scan the checks themselves and the bank then sends the image to the clearing house.

I wish corporate customers could take the digital leap, but they cannot force their own clients to change purchase patterns. Their business nuances can make transformation very difficult.

Real estate developers still want to collect post-dated checks for property sales. Psychologically, businesses feel safer with checks as it provides legal remedy against non-payment. In Singapore, these situations carry a civil liability. Instead of being frustrated by the slow digital adoption, we prefer to work with the status quo and give customers a digital "taste test," moving them towards a better solution that uses new tools without forcing them to ditch cash and checks.

We have faith that, eventually, digital migration will happen. This might take another generation, or may need some change in legal consequences related to checks. But first, we need to build a bridge.

High-Touch versus High-Tech Banking

There is an accepted framework of high-touch versus high-tech in banking. For top customer tiers, banks can afford high-touch, i.e., have RMs (relationship managers) serve clients. And the lower tiers are product-managed using technology platforms for cost efficiency reasons.

But I heard new ways of looking at this paradigm.

1. Digitization can make RMs significantly more productive, and help them efficiently serve the middle customer tier with sufficient customization via personas or clusters. And we have top-tier customers who prefer to go digital than "verbal" banking for the mundane tasks.

2. Tech guys insist that they are not just high-tech. They propose that technology is how they touch people's lives, although in a different way. This is the point raised by Google's chief decision scientist. I agree as long as the CX design delights.

3. And then there are chatbots and robo advisers. I have met several of these companies. In theory, more customers can be served by a robo RM, although the lack of bot sophistication compared to the complexity of customer questions still leads to discontent. Customers prefer to talk to a person, especially if there is a service issue.

Recent research points to significant preference for human conversations as customers easily get frustrated with chat bots. The bet is that chatbot features will improve faster with GenAI. It is difficult to predict how this will look like in five or ten years. What I would do is bet on two plans. First, keep augmenting my sales force with AI, and second, keep a close eye on bot developments.

Part Four

Get a Life

”

The end of work is not death. The end of work is more life.

Chapter Eleven

Don't Die Twice

I am defined as a banker. Almost everyone knows me as such, even if there is more to me than work. Work consumes me.

Before it completely takes over, make sure there is more to your life than the desk and the laptop that owns you every Monday morning. Your health, your hobbies, your food choices, your books, your style, your experiences, your advocacies, your friends, your family. They should continue to be a big part of you because, at some point, work will stop.

I watched Roger Federer's retirement video where the stark reminder was: "Athletes die twice."

The end of work is not death. The end of work is more life.

Make Gym a Priority

Our gym is usually full soon after the holidays, as both locals and expats come back from their trips. Penance from too much drinking and eating is prescribed even for the agnostics.

Then attendance slows down after a couple of months as people forget their resolutions, and picks up in time for the beach season. During the lean months, only my regular "classmates" remain.

Over the last few years, I have learned that, for exercise to be consistent, you have to write it into your diary. For example, block TThS 6am for exercise. Avoid canceling or postponing. This is much like defining expenses as "salary minus savings." You work only after you exercise, with some exceptions, of course.

No pain, you gain!

There are days when I don't want to go. And there are times when I joke with my trainer that I should be paid for doing manual labor. This morning, on the treadmill, I listened to disco music expecting standard hits. It was a surprise that the next piece was a local favorite which brought back sentimental memories of the '70s, and the realization that I still can't dance the swing.

I repeated the piece five times to remind myself that I was, well, incomplete.

I am tired of watching others dance while I wonder why I still can't. How difficult can it be? I have enough thick skin to sing in front of hundreds. Played the sax even.

But dance?

Fasting and Fast Eating

When I crossed 50 years of age and spent eight weeks facing Harvard cases and the mess hall buffet spread, I gained weight. This was despite regular exercise and the cold weather. My suits started to shrink after two weeks.

Must be those study group meetings. We munched nuts during those times. Beer was also readily available. And lobsters! I fixed the problem by reducing my food intake and avoiding carbs. I was already familiar with the low-carb diet, and did it for a short period only following doctor's advice. I slimmed down in time for graduation.

At 60, weight loss is torture. I also realized that my eating habits deteriorate when I am unhappy or stressed. But there is nothing like very tight pants and suits, and a prominent double chin to put me in panic mode.

You cannot face the problem if the problem is your face.

What works for me is a combination of exercise and cardio, low-carb for three weeks, and intermittent fasting (eight hours feeding) five times a week. Breakfast has more vegetables than meat or fish. Fasting is tricky because, as bankers, we get invited by clients. So we do the best we can.

I am beginning to feel like an accordion. Sometimes wide, sometimes narrow. That being the case, I measure my weight using a reliable pair of blue pants. When I fit comfortably, I'm okay. Consult your doctor before you choose which scheme to commit to. Luckily, my wife is a physician and wellness expert so I get free advice.

Two Balls, One Heavier than the Other

Where I grew up, we took duckpin bowling seriously. We used smaller balls so it was child-friendly. Then I came to Manila where, for some, ten-pin bowling is a religion. Switching to bigger balls wasn't that hard. I just had to add one more step to my approach.

It was probably a mistake to join my former bank's team, as being watched tensed up my body, and the balls did not roll as intended. It was mental for sure, mostly because of the overthinking of the physics behind the game.

Bowling was supposed to be enjoyable. In a team, it was quite the opposite. The only fun part about bowling was the eating and drinking — nachos, sausages, pizza, and beer.

There was this added burden of carrying a bag that contained my shoes and other equipment. I had to explain to the unskilled why we needed two balls. The first was heavier so that the momentum was strong enough to drop 10 pins. The second was lighter, for targeted hunting of spares. I often just needed to hit one to four remaining stubborn pins.

They key to good performance is practice. I devoted a few hours every weekend for this. It was time consuming. What kept me going was the possibility that our team will win. And we did. As soon as I won my first high game trophy, mostly because of luck, I knew I had to retire from competition.

The trophy is still there on my shelves, in a prominent place. I quit while I was ahead.

Cleaning Up

Last year during Easter week, Good Friday in particular, I went to Church's in Hong Kong. This year, I stayed home and, for atonement, attacked my closet and the library. They needed to be reorganized.

I have a habit of culling. I cull files, magazines, and papers in the office quarterly, and cull clothes annually. I give away old stuff to make room for new ones.

The books we removed were donated to those who can still use them. The ones that were no longer relevant were picked up by recyclers. I still have a dozen new ones, all gifts, I haven't even removed the plastic.

We had old editions and banking manuals which we didn't want to discard in case we would still need them in the future. At 60, I finally bade them goodbye.

But my (and my family's) favorites will remain treasured, and will keep their prominent positions on the shelves. These include plenty of children's books, British history, and other good reads that I imagine I will be enjoying even in my 70s.

Why British history? I am not entirely sure. Maybe because my father liked to lecture about the Disraeli and Gladstone rivalry. Maybe because my boys studied there. Better yet, it is more satisfying "shopping" from my pile of old clothes, especially when I fit into my old favorites. It beats shopping in the malls or the Internet! It gives me a high that only other senior citizens will understand.

I always keep the clothes I really like. I am hoping that sometime in the future, when I miraculously shed 15 pounds, I will fit into them again.

Imitation Topsiders

When I was teaching in the mid-'80s, I did not realize how upper-class many students were. For a public university, we had too many cars, and I was sure they were mostly not driven by teachers. In fact, parking was already a problem.

It made me think about disparities in high school preparations as my students were, for the most part, from exclusive Manila schools and the elite Philippine Science High School. This inequality still exists up to this day. Although the expansion of the Science High School system to 16 campuses, and 17 other regional science-specialized schools has helped.

The gap was most apparent in footwear. Top-siders, often worn with argyles and colorful socks, versus imitation boat shoes from local factories. I had students who had Sperry top-siders in several colors so they could match their OOTD (outfit of the day).

I had one in beige, made in Marikina. And everyone could see that it was the cheap version as I always stood on a platform when teaching. When you can't afford, you manage within the affordable price points. I alternated it with rubber shoes. I wore them with confidence.

My pair survived grad school and my early years at Citi. They were durable and value for money, even if the sole was a bit soft. The bottom curved up like a boat.

Boat shoes, indeed.

By this time, you know I have a fondness for shoes. I still remember where I got my pairs when I was still starting. They were from a shop called "Bristol," a local brand. Every year, I still pass by their shop to check their stocks.

The Nose Knows

I read somewhere that the nose might be the fastest sense. The whole brain gets fired up when familiar scents enter our nostrils. Our neurons are wired in a way that gives smell a shortcut to the center of our brain, bypassing many layers.

Like freshly baked bread. It brings me back to my childhood. Maybe that is why I like holding interviews in a bakeshop. It sets the mood right. I once worked in a building that had a bakery on the ground floor. Entering the lobby was always a pleasant experience.

Like the salty breeze from the sea. Like freshly cut grass. Like new books. Like strawberry ice cream. Like coffee in the morning. It perks me up even before I sip from the cup. Like a glass of whisky, gin, or wine.

We should not forget how the sense of smell immediately changes our mood and our perception of the environment.

Have you noticed how your grandma used to kiss you? Mine pressed her nose against my cheek. Other cultures have the same practice. The inuits call this gesture a "kunik." The irony though is, while I like certain scents, I avoid using cologne as it feels unnatural. I still have a dozen unopened bottles.

The best smells in my memory are of my two boys when they were babies. I spent hours sniffing them while they were sleeping. They are in their 20s now (and their officemates might read this post and tease them).

I also do the same thing with my cats, even if they find it annoying sometimes.

Daddy's nose never forgets.

Breaking Fast

Have you ever been amazed at how your breakfast patterns changed?

As a kid, my favorite was fried egg, fried rice, and two pieces of Vienna sausage which came from a can with eight pieces, split among four siblings. We had that once weekly, although it was usually fried fish most mornings. It was easy to prepare and consume.

By the time I went to college, the sausages were replaced with three small pieces of chorizo de Cebu. Now, every time I visit the city, I look for those sweet balls of meat in hotel buffets. I get disappointed when I don't see them.

In grad school, on a tight budget, it was always an egg sandwich, cooked expertly as I watched and waited, and pitch-black coffee.

In my first year at AIM, a McDonalds opened right across the street. I never had breakfast there as I couldn't afford the extra expense.

As a young trader, my quick meal had two pieces of choco butternut donuts and coffee from Dunkin Donuts. When a coffee shop opened at Citi, the donut surrendered its place to blueberry muffin. I continued that practice in Hong Kong.

When traveling, the hotels seem to have the same menu globally. I avoid anything garlicky as I am in meetings the whole day.

Now, I particularly enjoy granola and yogurt every now and then. Or a plate of bitter melon with egg, without rice, with decaf coffee in the mornings. I don't need caffeine until later at 10am.

What starts your day?

Going Local in Singapore

Char kway teow and white carrot cake. Prawn mee and *bak kut teh*. I ate local food mostly in the non-tourist spots in Singapore. It was the best way to get to know the place and its people, beyond ordering chicken rice and satay at Newton Circus, or chili and pepper crab at East Coast or No Signboard.

I owe it to Eric Sim, my Singaporean buddy and author of the best-selling book *Small Actions*, who showed me around.

During lunch breaks or late in the afternoon, we would hop into his sleek Audi, and do our eating meetings on the road. We discussed business while he introduced me to local dishes.

I cannot forget *rojak*, a salad of fruits and veggies with a sweet and sour sauce, which has no equivalent anywhere in the world. It was hard to focus on the topic at hand when a plate of *rojak* was between us.

I tried other dishes as well. I have become a self-proclaimed expert on beef rendang, an Indonesian dish that is popular in Singapore as well. And the conveyor belt sushi places looked so innovative that my family went to them weekly.

I enjoyed those outings far more than the sit-down dinners in fancy restaurants.

When we did not have time to go out, we rushed to the food court next door before legions of programmers from the next building came out in droves. I went Indian, Korean, or Filipino, depending on where the queue was shorter.

When in Singapore, avoid the tourist traps and eat where the locals go. If you know Sim Boon Chye, you are in luck. Can, lah!

Eating Local in Manila

When your Filipino friends show you around Manila, you get to try *lechon* (roast pig). If your friends are naughty, they will trick you into eating *balut* (duck embryo) or durian, the fruit that smells like hell but tastes like heaven.

If you are with me, I will make you taste *sisig*. It is hard to describe the dish except to say it comes in a hot metal plate and is made from chopped parts of a pig's head. Legend has it that a cook saw hundreds of that part of the pig being discarded at Clark Air Base kitchens. She saw dollars in those heads.

There are rules in eating *sisig*. First, never serve it with egg. And second, absolutely no mayonnaise on top. Those from Central Luzon are purists about protecting their dish. Down it with local beer.

My favorite lunch is a vegetable dish called crispy *pinakbet*. I often have it three lunches in a row. Even five. Always without rice and with less squash, and more green stuff — okra, eggplant, string beans, and bitter melon. And crispy pork.

I consider it the perfect low-carb meal, although nutritionists will probably beg to differ. The innocence from the veggies overwhelms the guilt from the pork, although someone wrote that pork fat is a good source of monounsaturated fats. Okay, the guilt is unsaturated.

As a child, I had to be cajoled into eating vegetables. I changed my mind when I spent several days in an agricultural college where the mess hall served the freshest vegetables. I have been hooked since then.

My colleagues are amused by my choice, but some now order the same.

Got the Moves Like Jagger

Recently, I had dinner with an old schoolmate who is two years ahead of me. I had not seen him for over four decades. He majored in engineering, worked in a bank, after which he migrated to a foreign country. When he sent me a note to catch up, I put it high on my agenda.

Why?

Because back in high school, he was one of my idols. He had the moves like Jagger and was always seen with the prettiest girl. He also had a piano-playing classmate who was similarly skilled. Younger boys like me watched the two masters at their game.

We finally had a chance to summarize the last 45 years. Talked about family, classmates, common friends, and school. It is true — the older you get, the stronger the urge to reconnect with people you grew up with.

I told him where everyone we knew was and what they were doing. He did the same. Meetings like this bring me back to high school.

I now try to spend as much time as I can with my close friends from high school and university. I find time during business trips. There is no feeling quite like the affection and acceptance that grew over half a century. Those friendships, as my favorite group sang, "never end!"

And yes, about Jagger, I was actually in a Hong Kong bar and sat 10 meters away from him. It was dimly lit, unfortunately.

So what did I learn? Please don't start me up. If you start me up, I'll never stop. (Lines from Maroon 5 and Rolling Stones)

Hungry Like the Wolf

I am not exactly a music enthusiast, even if I sometimes sing parts of my slides during presentations. In the car while on the way to work, I don't listen to music. I do emails instead.

But I often play U2 when I am driving alone. Sadly, I forget the playlist after three songs as my mind shifts to other thoughts. I don't have a Spotify subscription.

In college in the '80s, I rarely missed *American Top 40*. I always knew which songs were trending, and they still play in my head. Like Toto singing *Africa* which I kept humming in Nairobi. I mostly missed the new bands post-2000 and had to be educated on Maroon 5 and Coldplay. And Taylor Swift. I quite like her "Love Story" even if I am more fond of the theme song from the movie of the same title from 1971.

But I stop what I am doing when I hear Duran Duran's *Hungry Like a Wolf*, *Save a Prayer*, *New Moon on Monday*, etc. Especially *Rio*! And Pet Shop Boys' *Rent*, *Always on My Mind*, and *West End Girls*. I sing along.

And Bon Jovi. I ended a speech recently with a memorable line about being hit in the heart and how love was to blame.

Whenever I visit my favorite Spanish restaurant, I ask the guitar trio to play *Hotel California* using their acoustic guitars. I check them out every time I like, but I can always leave.

One time, in between jobs, I tried to learn how to play the guitar. I had sax lessons as well. Both did not prosper.

Advocating for Santa Claus

We used to prepare cookies and milk, and eat part of a cookie afterwards to pretend Santa passed by. I had to do this carefully because my boys started to become skeptical early on, even if they enjoyed their gifts.

We even had to send an email to Santaclaus@northpole.com (I made this up) so my elder son's request for a medium-sized brown teddy bear would be submitted promptly. I later found a Santa email address that responded, complete with "Ho, ho, ho!" I printed Santa's reply and my elder son was amazed.

We were not flawless. We argued why Santa used gift-wrapping paper from Borders, that he outsourced the wrapping to parents because he did not have time to do it. The teddy bear used up quite a lot of paper, you see.

I admit it was fun, although every year my wife and I gradually lost our case. I don't even remember how the Santa ritual ended.

There was another ritual that I enjoyed, that did not have integrity concerns. It was the Christmas star project of my elder son. My wife and I spent hours making sure he had the best-looking star.

As parents, we had to keep the two babies entertained, astonished, and suspicious in their early years. Apart from Santa, there were vacations to the usual fun places, hours at the toy and book stores, and trips to the beach. Now they are much bigger and, at the last beach we went to, they matched my rum intake.

Family traditions, even if irrational, are immensely enjoyable.

”

Bankers can’t be rebels at work, so I practice insurgency while sipping.

Chapter Twelve

You Need a Drink

I have been categorized as a whisky drinker. As a result, my stocks are replenished during my birthday and the Christmas season. This was not always the case. Before this, I got bottles of wine.

I did what nerds always do. I bought a book about wine, and studied the first dozen I ever had to understand the grapes, where they were grown, and the fermentation process. I later did the same for my whisky stash. I intellectualized the drink.

A Rebel on the Rum

My entry into post-beer alcohol was gin, Ginebra San Miguel in small sips, while studying at the dormitory. We flavored it with a bit of lemon, and chased it down with water. When my friend Peter Paul opened a bottle of London Dry, it was deceptively safe until I couldn't stand straight afterwards.

While I didn't have gin regularly, the Aboitiz Txanton 150 Acorns version tasted heavenly and brought back memories. I quietly consumed that bottle and the next, a few sips at a time. Endika told me to holler if I needed to replenish. Maybe I will do this soon.

There are a few more local brands, notably ARC, that have made their mark. It is a pity that I missed the chance to visit their distillery.

Today, marketers have convinced me that I should be drinking aged whisky from the Scotland Glens or Highlands (which has a princely ring to it). I tried to educate myself and even read about the type of charred oak barrels that were used, and if those barrels were new or old. Old oak barrels were previously used to age sherry, bourbon, and wine. If sherry, was it Oloroso?

To be fair, I have enjoyed the multi-sensory experience. But after drinking from 100 bottles (sips, not the whole 750ml), I have decided I don't prefer Macallan, although I have been gifted 12s, 15s, and a couple of 18s. Maybe because of the TV series *Suits*, the brand remains quite popular among my colleagues. I struggle to finish them as I find the older ones too smooth.

The same goes for Yamazaki and Hibiki, although I still remember, very distinctly, a rare Yamazaki 25 from the Osaka distillery. It is still the best I have ever tasted. No contest.

Instead, I have found smokey or peaty whiskies thrilling. After I tried Lagavulin 16 upon Manolet Salak's urging, I never turned back and even begged for more. I found Laphroaig, Ardbeg, and Octomore. Apologies for the rhyme. Johnnie Double Black turned out to have some peatiness.

It seems that I go for a bit of attitude. Bankers can't be rebels at work, so I practice insurgency while sipping.

When seeking a drink that is slightly tame, I prefer Glenfiddich 18 or a Dalmore.

One of my Indian friends brought me a bottle, and asked how it tasted. The Indian brand was unique. It was like a Mac 12 at the start, but had a sweet finish. When I checked the box, it indicated that the alcohol was aged in oak barrels, and later in casks that used to hold red wine. Interesting.

A couple of weeks ago, my nephew brought me a 4-year old Kentucky bourbon, a bottle of New Riff. I immediately opened it for a shot when I got home, careful to let it air first, otherwise I would burn my nostrils. I declared that it was distantly related to its peaty cousins in Scotland, a very good find, full of flavor.

Last Christmas, I finally discovered rum. Those who know me in college remember me wearing a brown rum shirt, but I never drank the brand. That is one regret that I have since corrected. Over 10 days, I always ordered rum and never touched whisky. Admittedly, seeing a bottle from Barbados labeled ESA Field made me biased.

I also found out that Mount Gay Rum was the first drink Daniel Craig ordered as 007. Naturally, I have a bottle of that as well. It is the second best thing from Barbados, after the fascinating Rihanna.

A Whisky Masterclass Plus More

How often can one have an intense discussion on whisky with the owner of a leading distillery? Rarely.

One evening, I got lucky. Dr. Andrew Tan was at the same event I attended. I started by sharing that my family went to Glasgow and we passed by the Dalmore House. The tycoon smiled and told me that he would arrange a distillery visit next time. Soon, we were into half an hour of whisky history, sherry casks, and even types of rum.

In summary, blended whisky is a mix of various whiskies and neutral spirits. Single malt is malt whisky from a single distillery. What makes his brands special is the aging process in used sherry casks like Oloroso and Ximenez which impart spicy, fruity, chocolatey, and nutty attributes to the liquid over time.

Access to sherry casks is of existential importance in this industry. Many years ago, when his purchase of the largest brandy company was announced, what piqued my curiosity was the sherry business that came along with the acquisition. Very strategic.

Finally, we moved to cognac and rum where he made a distinction between mixing and sipping rums.

I did not count on being lucky twice. A few months after the first chat, I met him again during his company's anniversary celebration. I sat next to Lou Gutierrez-Alfonso who was announced that morning as the new president of Megaworld, Dr. Tan's real estate arm. The special menu suggested pairing dishes with brandy. That was totally new, and of course I tried it.

The Fundador Supremo 18, which was aged in Oloroso sherry casks, brilliantly matched the richness of the soup. It got even better when we tried the next dishes.

Whiskey Physics: Scotch on a Rock

I came across an article which delightfully explains why the Japanese owner of Lit, the whiskey joint near my condo, carefully carves ice balls while standing behind the bar.

It is all about, you guessed it, physics! On heat transfer and the ball having a smaller surface area than what an equivalent mass of cubes have. Of course, it is part showmanship which, admittedly, works! The bar is, after all, quite popular.

I prefer my whisky neat, which means no ice. But I like to add a tiny bit of water. According to chemists, at 40% alcohol, the "flavor-carrying molecules" tend to stay below the surface of the liquid, trapped beneath the surface tension. A drop or two of water literally opens up the drink and releases the aromas promised on the backside of the bottle.

This technical explanation never fails to impress fellow drinkers. Why don't you share a bit of science the next time you are in the bar?

And finally, physicists who were probably taking a break from quantum mechanics found out that whiskeys leave signature patterns at the bottom of the glass. These patterns were uniform coffee ring type for American brands which use new oak barrels, but were more understandably complicated for Scotch which are aged in used casks. These patterns provide a unique "fingerprint" for whisky brands and ages, and can be used to detect fraud.

In conclusion, all these confirm why I chose the right drink. And the correct way to consume it.

Whiskey webs: Microscale "fingerprints" of bourbon whiskey. Stuart J. Williams, Martin J. Brown, VI, and Adam D. Carrithers. Phys. Rev. Fluids 4, 100511. Published 24 October 2019.

Appreciating Alcohol

I avoid writing about wine because it is a complicated topic complete with real experts. I suggest you read about it in wine books instead, or watch YouTube videos. I will keep this short.

I follow simple rules — when eating fish or salads, I choose white wine. Usually a Riesling from the Alsace region, or Sauvignon Blanc from New Zealand's Marlborough district. Any brand from these places will do. Or I compromise on a Chardonnay, chilled.

With meat, I pick Malbec or Shiraz. And then any of the Italian and Spanish reds. The restaurant can suggest a pairing, such as matching a full-bodied wine with a rich meal. I often deviate from this rule, especially when I want to focus on the dishes. I pick a lighter wine.

I am sure my choices are not the best, but I just learned to like them and their friendly price points.

By the way, I suggest you appreciate the effort winemakers (and distillers) put into their craft. Lift the glass to appreciate the color; it can suggest what types of barrels were used to age the alcohol. Slowly twirl the glass and notice how some of the liquid clings to the sides. Take a sniff and imagine what it reminds you of. Winemakers can be very creative with their descriptions.

Then take a sip and use it to coat parts of your tongue and mouth. Let your imagination run wild. Only then should you actually start swallowing, but pay attention to the aftertaste.

The same steps apply to whisky, except that you need to be careful when inhaling a pour from a freshly opened bottle.

Cheers!

More Than Just Coffee

I take my coffee black, without sugar.

Coffee to me used to be just what it is, a dark drink with a bitter taste that I enjoy, often with breakfast or snacks. In fact, when traveling around the provinces in the past, I had the habit of bringing single-serve Nescafé packets because, otherwise, my hosts would offer me a three-in-one.

I was consistent. Black coffee. Smokey whiskey taken neat. Dark chocolate. And dark beer/stout.

And then the coffee industry made my life complicated and raised the beverage into a multi-sensory experience.

I had a machine in my old office where I poured some Arabica beans into a cavity, listened intently while the beans were ground, watched with awe while the liquid trickled into my cup, admired the thin layer of crema formed by minute bubbles of coffee oil, inhaled slowly as the bubbles started popping. This is when I counted myself lucky. Then, I sip and get on with work.

In my office, for convenience, I have a Nespresso. The experience is not as comprehensive, but I get to partially enjoy the visual and aromatic treat. When on Zoom, I put my laptop on mute while I insert a capsule into the machine. The transparent glass cups allow me to examine the crema while I listen to insights from my teammates.

Lately, I bought coconut-flavored capsules. The aroma of coconuts filled the office, reminding me of macaroons and time spent on the farm as a young boy.

”

Cats have very different personalities. Even if they were raised at the same time in the same environment, their uniqueness will clearly show.

Chapter Thirteen

Pet Shop Boy

We have 14 pets: 3 tortoises, 2 dogs, and 9 cats. Quantitatively speaking, I am more of a cat person.

Having an enjoyably stressful job requires massive sources of compensating happy hormones. Gym is one source, the pool is another. And since our boys are off on their adult adventures, my wife and I spend much time hanging around our cats. They shower us with snobby affection, nagging demands for food, and random cuddles, all without the need to take them out for a walk.

Cat Thermodynamics

My cat Hammhamm feels very warm, like he is forever having a flu. I had to research this phenomenon the first time I had him. The hairlessness of his breed (Sphynx) means that they have no insulation, and have difficulty retaining heat. More calories burned makes more heat. This is what makes him different from normal furry cats.

The Sphynx is also very warm, as in very friendly. They love being cuddled. More affectionate than dogs, they are often mistaken for puppies. Whenever I take Hamm out to the vet, those who see him argue whether he is a cat or dog.

His skin tends to be greasy. We know where he spends time the most because he leaves a reddish oily stain. Goodbye, white walls.

Hamm was a gift from Rina Ortiz who knew I loved cats. When I went over to pick Hamm up, I saw that she had over two dozen hairless cats.

He was named after Dag Hammarskjöld, the late UN Secretary-General who is my younger son's idol. Except that he is a cat, Cat Hammarskjöld. He tries to be diplomatic, although it does not work on other cats who can't figure out whether he is one of them.

He might be an intellectual as he spends most of his time in the library, on top of books, usually at the very top shelves. I know because the books are stained.

Hamm was once featured in a local magazine website *Bilyonaryo*, I don't know why. He does not have a penny to his name.

But for a while, he was a "hot item."

Unconditional Love From My Pet Crackers

Crackers has been a constant source of affection for the past 15 years. As a Bichon Frise, he may be small in size, but his love knows no bounds.

Crackers came into our lives as the offspring of our first pet Fuzzy and our neighbor's dog, Chanel. We named him after a Thai dessert, rice crackers with pork floss, but it was clear that he is much more than just a sweet treat.

Despite our initial plan to sell him, we quickly changed our minds when we first saw and carried him. How could we part with such a wonderful cuddly ball? He must have remembered that I was so adamant to keep him.

I am honored to be his favorite human. When he was younger, he would run to the kitchen upon hearing my voice, wagging his tail and demanding cuddles. He always made me feel welcome, although it came with certain obligations.

To repay his affection, I would give him neck massages, and on weekends he would find me and nudge my feet until I complied. That stopped whatever I was doing as he demanded attention.

When my sons were younger, Crackers slept with them, often sharing a pillow.

Even in his old age, when he can no longer see and his hearing is impaired, he still roams the house as if he had mapped it in his brain.

A month ago, I canceled my afternoon meetings and rushed to the pet hospital when I found out he was unwell and in pain. Thankfully, it was just one of those old-age afflictions. He was soon back to his roaming routine.

Conditional Love

While my dog Crackers showers me with loyal affection, I don't get the same from our cat, Georgia. She is our only female cat, and it looks like she knows it.

She is the mother of Yale, Prince, and Harvey, collectively known as the Ivy cats (they were born when I was in Boston). She is exclusively loyal to my elder son, her rescuer, the only object of her absolute affection. She often waits outside my son's room if she sees movement inside.

Sherlock is her sleeping companion. They are often curled together at night. They get along well although it is clear who "wears the pants."

I had to win her trust over many months of calling her name and staying close to her. Eventually, she started rubbing against my feet. She is hard to catch, but easy to trap when sleepy. When she is stuck with me, or when no one else is home, she demands neck and belly rubs, making sure I am useful.

I now get to kiss her, and she does not run away when I do. She even purrs and I call her my baby girl. I just need to make sure she is in the right mood.

I am convinced she can understand when I tell her I should be her favorite person from now on. Except that she does not agree.

I can't help but smile whenever I see her when I get home. Her snobbish ways and blue eyes have a way of removing my stress.

She is turning 11 this year.

My Pussycat Schrödinger's Experiment

Every physics student that has been paying attention must have heard of Schrödinger's cat experiment. (Google it.) That is why one of my cats had to be named Schrö. My friends never failed to remind me to do so.

Just like my other cat Morgan, named after John Pierpont, Schrö was left by his biological mom in the ceiling. They got through a small hole on the side of the roof. For days we could hear crying and whimpering, until we found a way to get to him. (We ended up breaking part of the ceiling.)

As a baby, he was very sweet and confident. His first nickname was Schröberry. His curiosity led to him tinkering with anything, including the dogs who were quite patient with him. He would strut around the house all day or be sleeping.

As he got bigger, the sweetness diminished and the confidence grew. You can say that he has become quite bossy, and he still goes around surveying his property. He is not friendly at all, but he isn't wild.

Cats, indeed, have very different personalities. Even if they were raised at the same time in the same environment, their uniqueness will clearly show.

It does matter when we got them. If they were on the streets fending for themselves for weeks before we adopted them, it took long before they lost their wild side.

Of our nine cats, no two have the same traits.

Why nine? Nine lives? Actually, it just happened.

Georgia and Oxytocin

Georgia is a great source of oxytocin. And cuddling her, although she requires much convincing, lowers the blood pressure.

My elder son found her hiding in fear under the car hood when the two puppies were chasing her. She must have been two months old when we got her, so she retains a bit of her skeptical side. She then became a boarder in my elder son's room for years.

In the office, we sometimes discuss who the dog lovers are and who prefers cats. Each side has their reasons. The anti-cats stress that cats are not affectionate. The pro-cats love that their pets take care of their own hygiene, and do not have to be brought out to do their numbers one and two.

I read that cat lovers tend to be introverts, curious, and sensitive. Just like their pets. I love my dogs too, which says that I am also extroverted. Maybe I am both, or in the middle of the intro-extrovert spectrum. Or just confused.

Cats are quite independent but also loyal. And that loyalty has to be earned and is not freely given. With water, food, litter box, and some soft cloth, they are content. Unfortunately, they scratch the furniture. By scratch, I mean "destroy." A cat person must literally make the decision: cat or furniture. I chose cat. The only downside is when they accidentally pee outside their litter box. The smell is horrible.

I must have been a well-behaved human because, lately, Georgia has been watching me while I set off to work.

Or maybe it means good riddance.

”

The ability of Singapore to transform in a single generation through quality education was incredibly impressive. A real proof of concept. That influenced why education remains my main advocacy, and I serve in three school boards.

Chapter Fourteen

Disastrous and Delightful

In this chapter, I will share some career highlights that I cannot forget. Some were disastrous, others delightful. I have kept repeating these stories up to this day.

I write about my best and worst trips, my most inspiring incidents, and those that scared me. The extremes have influenced my view of people and places.

I count myself lucky that a young man from a remote province in Mindanao had the chance to see the world, its splendor and its faults, and was enriched by the experience.

Near Death from Horrible Hotel Service

In 2009, I went to New York for a series of meetings and stayed in a hotel (which I will not name). That evening, I treated two friends to dinner and ordered lamb chops.

The next morning, as my tummy was churning violently, I called the hotel staff for help. A doctor came and I was promptly charged $400 for the house call. A hundred per minute, but at least I had a prescription.

As I could barely stand, and seeing that there was a drugstore across the road from my window, I requested assistance again from the concierge to buy medicine. They refused because of some legal BS.

Fortunately, I was able to call a friend who brought Gatorade, bananas, and crackers, and walked across to get the meds. I remain eternally grateful to her.

I then wrote an email to the hotel manager warning them that a childhood friend was a doctor-administrator with the NY Department of Health, and I could have their license confiscated. I had all my meals in the hotel, hence they were the only source of food poisoning. And I reminded them that I was a managing director of Citi, and could have their accreditation delisted, pronto.

At least they immediately wrote back apologizing and reversing all charges, including the dinner and doctor's charge. I paid nothing. When I got back to Hong Kong, I received another letter from the general manager. What remained was the really nasty aftertaste of experiencing the worst customer service ever.

This incident made me more sensitive to customers' needs, especially during anxious moments.

Four Weeks in Citi London

One of my best memories with Citi was my foreign exchange audit assignment in London.

My hotel was the InterContinental Park Lane located right across Hyde Park. The other side faced the Duke of Wellington Memorial. Buckingham Palace was a short walk away, less than 10 minutes.

I reported to the office at the Strand, the business district before banks moved to Canary Wharf. It was easy to get to as the Hyde Park Corner Underground Station was, as stated, right around the corner, and the stop was Charing Cross. The old Citi headquarters was quite traditional-looking, as were all the other buildings in "The City."

Some days, I had to do fieldwork at Lewisham, which took around 45 minutes to get to via the Victoria Station. Most of the trip was on a regular train, above ground. It felt rural to some extent.

I lugged around a heavy IBM ThinkPad and tried to fit in. This was when I discovered bowties, and I wore them most days looking very much like an auditor.

I noticed people ate sandwiches in the offices and I did the same. Coffee came from a vendo machine. To fill my stomach with real food, my colleague Jackson Pak brought me to Chinatown.

As the sun set quite late, I visited as many museums as I could, walked in the parks, and took a train to Cambridge. It was cold and I wore an oversized, borrowed coat.

It was serious work, but serious fun at the same time. That made me appreciate new cultures more, and London became my favorite city after that.

Singapore and the Power of Education

In 2001, Citi Treasury management created a new Regional Derivatives Structuring and Sales Team based in Singapore. And I was going to lead it.

Under me was a former member of the Australian gymnastics team who headed options, an engineer who ran risk advisory, and a crew of senior transactors doing derivatives — from Harvard, Oxford, and Singapore universities. (The gymnast later founded Gilmour Space Corporation; the engineer has become a best-selling author.)

For three years, we were suitcase bankers. We were in Changi Airport almost every week and made friends around Asia.

I deeply admired my Singaporean colleagues because they were talented and they worked really hard. Most of them came from humble backgrounds, benefiting from the education policies of Lee Kuan Yew. They were very strong in math, english, and sciences.

My head of risk advisory, for instance, used to help at his father's prawn noodle stall in a hawker center. The father-in-law of one of my structurers was the master cutter of the best tailoring shop along Tanglin. One of my structurers wrote so beautifully in English that I called him Shakespeare.

The ability of the country to transform in a single generation through quality education was incredibly impressive. A real proof of concept. That influenced why education remains my main advocacy, and I serve in three school boards.

I am grateful to AIM President Jikyeong Kang for recruiting me to the board, to Father Miranda for considering me worthy to be a trustee in my alma mater, and to Brother Felipe for appointing me to lead my high school's executive and finance committees.

Citi Hong Kong Scare

My Citi Hong Kong team made me feel at home even if I did not speak the language. I tried to take lessons, but the only thing left is my being able to utter "I don't understand Cantonese," but in Cantonese.

The Hong Kong treasury seniors were old friends of mine. My secretary was an extremely efficient lady who spoiled me with glazed egg tarts. I also had fresh daisies every Monday. (Yellow daisies and white roses remain my favorite.)

My team liked to eat as Hong Kong has great cuisine. Since we did a lot of walking anyway, we burned lunch quickly. Whenever fish was served, the boss had to finish off the fish head. I became quite an expert in that.

But before I could be "permanent," I had to pass the dreaded Paper 1 (for financial markets participants) and Paper 2 (for managers) exams given by the regulator. One of my traders warned me that many had to take the exams twice or thrice.

Everyone on the floor knew that I needed to hurdle this requirement. I was under so much pressure. It was a moment of truth!

I locked myself up in my office and spent hours reading, reviewing, and taking two mock exams until I felt confident. On the exam date, as I took two exams that morning, my vision was hazy by lunchtime.

A week later, my name showed up on the website's honor list. I was greatly relieved. I printed the page and framed it. It remains the only set of government licenses that I had to take to exercise my profession.

Remembering the Global Financial Crisis (GFC)

When I moved to lead the Hong Kong trading room in late 2006, the financial markets were just starting to be eventful. Bear Sterns was acquired by JPMorgan. Then Lehman went under. As they were the main counterparties for equity derivatives, it was handy to have my friends in Citigroup Equity Derivatives helping me out by taking over contracts originally held by Lehman.

Every day, I was watching the credit default swap (CDS) prices for my counterparties, looking for hints of trouble. In November 2008, we had withdrawals on Thursday and Friday. I was home in Manila that Friday evening but decided to return to Hong Kong a day earlier, and called everyone to the office for a Sunday meeting to ensure we were ready for Monday.

Thankfully, the Fed intervened Monday lunchtime (Sunday in the States). Unfortunately, the cost-cutting measures were going to be even tighter.

During a crisis, I follow a few simple rules: first, keep cash with note issuers or with the Central Bank. Second, be liquid. Third, watch the swap settlement counterparties especially if you pay in an earlier time zone.

I learned how important consumer deposits were, and how corporate and private banking deposits were more sensitive to reputational risk. With digital transactions, customers do not need to go to the branch.

The biggest damage was to our stock price. As we received stocks as part of our bonuses, someone joked before that we should imagine as if it had zero value. The joke wasn't funny any longer as the shares collapsed to low single digits. It hurt very badly those who never sold their shares beforehand.

A difficult time to forget.

”

The extremes have influenced my view of people and places.

What Comes Next?

I was asked twice recently.

In the first session, I replied that it ceased to be about me over 15 years ago. Once I discovered mentorship, it gradually became about the young leaders in my care. So my next big thing is to organize a leadership development program based on this book. From a personal standpoint, it is about my two boys and the careers they have chosen.

In the second, I recalled daydreaming while in the halls of the Asian Institute of Management, listening to a Citibank recruiter. I set two objectives that afternoon in 1986: to be country treasurer of the bank and be president of a local bank afterwards. I did the first in 2004, and the second happened in 2010. RCBC, which I started leading in 2019, has grown quite fast and this has created opportunities for our staff, the majority of whom are young breadwinners. For them, I feel a strong sense of duty. Business growth, therefore, continues to be a significant consideration.

The next big thing might be a third book on digital leadership. We shall see.

I am lucky I found my corner of the sky at the intersection of Ayala and Gil Puyat Avenues in Makati, Philippines, under the guidance of Mrs. Dee.

From there, I can fly.

Epilogue

Leadership is a trainable skill. Through this book, I hope I was able to mentor the reader virtually through the various skills, topics and stories, and help reinvent him/her to become a more effective leader.

Beyond this, it is my wish that this effectiveness translates into a higher level of performance for the team that the reader leads. And that he/she is able to harness new digital and data analytics tools to make his/her organization more competitive.

This will be for naught unless the leader looks for balance in his/her life, and finds purpose outside of work. Like any journey, life is best lived with people who support you and want you to succeed.

After completing this book, I was asked what my next plan was. My reply was that I will organize a leadership development program based on *Reinvention and Outperformance*. And seeing that there is a huge training gap in digital leadership, I will begin conducting research on this topic and prepare new material.

You will find me writing at my corner of the sky, at the intersection of Ayala and Gil Puyat Avenues, Makati Business District.

Yours ever,
Eugene

Index